Teach Yourself
VISUALLY™
Outlook® 2007

Visual

by Kate Shoup

D1410657

BICENTENNIAL
1807
WILEY
2007
BICENTENNIAL

Wiley Publishing, Inc.

Teach Yourself VISUALLY™ Outlook® 2007

Published by
Wiley Publishing, Inc.
111 River Street
Hoboken, NJ 07030-5774

Published simultaneously in Canada

Library of Congress Control Number: 2007926012

ISBN: 978-0-470-17124-0

Manufactured in the United States of America

10 9 8 7 6 5 4 3 2 1

Trademark Acknowledgments

Contact Us

For general information on our other products and services please contact our Customer Care Department within the U.S. at 800-762-2974, outside the U.S. at 317-572-3993, or fax 317-572-4002.

For technical support please visit www.wiley.com/techsupport.

Wiley Publishing, Inc.

Sales

Contact Wiley
at (800) 762-2974 or
fax (317) 572-4002.

Praise for Visual Books

"Like a lot of other people, I understand things best when I see them visually. Your books really make learning easy and life more fun."

John T. Frey (Cadillac, MI)

"I have quite a few of your Visual books and have been very pleased with all of them. I love the way the lessons are presented!"

Mary Jane Newman (Yorba Linda, CA)

"I just purchased my third Visual book (my first two are dog-eared now!), and, once again, your product has surpassed my expectations."

Tracey Moore (Memphis, TN)

"I am an avid fan of your Visual books. If I need to learn anything, I just buy one of your books and learn the topic in no time. Wonders! I have even trained my friends to give me Visual books as gifts."

Illona Bergstrom (Aventura, FL)

"Thank you for making it so clear. I appreciate it. I will buy many more Visual books."

J.P. Sangdong (North York, Ontario, Canada)

"I have several books from the Visual series and have always found them to be valuable resources."

Stephen P. Miller (Ballston Spa, NY)

"Thank you for the wonderful books you produce. It wasn't until I was an adult that I discovered how I learn – visually. Nothing compares to Visual books. I love the simple layout. I can just grab a book and use it at my computer, lesson by lesson. And I understand the material! You really know the way I think and learn. Thanks so much!"

Stacey Han (Avondale, AZ)

"I absolutely admire your company's work. Your books are terrific. The format is perfect, especially for visual learners like me. Keep them coming!"

Frederick A. Taylor, Jr. (New Port Richey, FL)

"I have several of your Visual books and they are the best I have ever used."

Stanley Clark (Crawfordville, FL)

"I bought my first Teach Yourself VISUALLY book last month. Wow. Now I want to learn everything in this easy format!"

Tom Vial (New York, NY)

"Thank you, thank you, thank you...for making it so easy for me to break into this high-tech world. I now own four of your books. I recommend them to anyone who is a beginner like myself."

Gay O'Donnell (Calgary, Alberta, Canada)

"I write to extend my thanks and appreciation for your books. They are clear, easy to follow, and straight to the point. Keep up the good work! I bought several of your books and they are just right! No regrets! I will always buy your books because they are the best."

Seward Kollie (Dakar, Senegal)

"Compliments to the chef!! Your books are extraordinary! Or, simply put, extra-ordinary, meaning way above the rest! THANK YOU THANK YOU THANK YOU! I buy them for friends, family, and colleagues."

Christine J. Manfrin (Castle Rock, CO)

"What fantastic teaching books you have produced! Congratulations to you and your staff. You deserve the Nobel Prize in Education in the Software category. Thanks for helping me understand computers."

Bruno Tonon (Melbourne, Australia)

"Over time, I have bought a number of your 'Read Less - Learn More' books. For me, they are THE way to learn anything easily. I learn easiest using your method of teaching."

José A. Mazón (Cuba, NY)

"I am an avid purchaser and reader of the Visual series, and they are the greatest computer books I've seen. The Visual books are perfect for people like myself who enjoy the computer, but want to know how to use it more efficiently. Your books have definitely given me a greater understanding of my computer, and have taught me to use it more effectively. Thank you very much for the hard work, effort, and dedication that you put into this series."

Alex Diaz (Las Vegas, NV)

Credits

Project Editor
Sarah Hellert

Acquisitions Editor
Jody Lefevere

Copy Editor
Kim Heusel

Technical Editor
James Floyd Kelly

Editorial Manager
Robyn Siesky

Editorial Assistant
Laura Sinise

Business Manager
Amy Knies

Manufacturing
Allan Conley
Linda Cook
Paul Gilchrist
Jennifer Guynn

Book Design
Kathie Rickard

Cover Design
Mike Trent

Production Coordinator
Erin Smith

Wiley Bicentennial Logo
Richard J. Pacifico

Layout
Carrie A. Foster
Jennifer Mayberry
Melanee Prendergast
Amanda Spagnuolo

Screen Artist
Jill A. Proll

Illustrators
Ronda David-Burroughs
Cheryl Grubbs
Shane Johnson

Proofreader
Melissa D. Buddendeck

Quality Control
Laura Albert
Brian Walls

Indexer
Sherry Massey

Special Help
Kit Malone
Barbara Moore

Vice President and Executive Group Publisher
Richard Swadley

Vice President and Publisher
Barry Pruett

Composition Director
Debbie Stailey

About the Author

During the course of her career as a freelance writer, **Kate Shoup** has written or co-written several books on various topics, including *Look & Learn FrontPage 2002*, *What Can You Do with a Major in Business*, *Not Your Mama's Beading*, *Not Your Mama's Stitching*, *Windows Vista Visual Encyclopedia*, and *Webster's New World English Grammar Handbook*. She has also co-written a screenplay, and worked as the Sports Editor for *NUVO Newsweekly*. Prior to striking out on her own, Kate worked as an editor at a computer-publishing company, where she engaged in such diverse professional activities as consulting on the development of new series, consulting on ways to improve the publishing workflow, and editing numerous standout titles. When not writing, Kate loves to ski (she was once nationally ranked), make jewelry, and play video poker — and she plays a mean game of 9-ball. Kate lives in Indianapolis, Indiana, with her daughter.

Author's Acknowledgments

The publication of any book is an enormous undertaking, involving many people, and this one is no exception. Thanks are due to Jody Lefevere for providing me with the opportunity to write this book, to Sarah Hellert for her expert guidance during the writing process, to Jim Kelly for his technical expertise, and to Kim Heusel for catching my numerous grammatical slip-ups. Thanks, too, to the book's graphics team — Ronda David-Burroughs, Cheryl Grubbs, Shane Johnson, Barbara Moore, Jill Proll, and Mike Trent. Thanks to the book's production team, composed of Laura Albert, Melissa Buddendeck, Sherry Massey, Jennifer Mayberry, Melanee Prendergast, Erin Smith, Amanda Spagnuolo, and Brian Walls. Finally, thanks to my family (especially my daughter Heidi) and friends — you know who you are.

Table of Contents

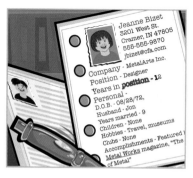

chapter 3 Organizing and Sharing Outlook Contacts

chapter 4 Handling Incoming E-mail

Table of Contents

chapter 5 Composing and Sending E-mail Messages

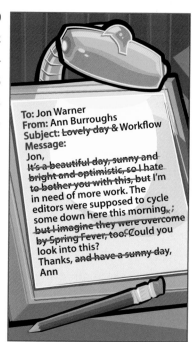

chapter 6 Text Messaging in Outlook

chapter 7 Using RSS Feeds

Table of Contents

chapter **8** Using the Outlook Calendar

chapter 9 Using Outlook's Task Component

chapter 10 Using Notes and Journal Entries

Table of Contents

chapter **11** **Managing Outlook**

chapter 12 Customizing Outlook

How to Use This Book

Do you look at the pictures in a book or newspaper before anything else on a page? Would you rather see an image instead of read about how to do something? Search no further. This book is for you. Opening *Teach Yourself VISUALLY Outlook 2007* allows you to read less and learn more about Outlook 2007.

Who Needs This Book

This book is for a reader who has never used this particular technology or software application. It is also for more computer-literate individuals who want to expand their knowledge of the different features that Outlook has to offer.

Book Organization

Teach Yourself VISUALLY Outlook 2007 is divided into 12 chapters, each of which teaches you a specific Outlook topic. If you have never used Outlook before, the first chapter gives you the basic techniques you require to get started. From there, each chapter is self-contained so that you can learn just the information you need at your own pace.

Chapter 1, **Exploring Outlook**, introduces the Outlook interface, as well as basic concepts and tools.

Chapter 2, **Creating and Using Outlook Contacts**, illustrates how you can use Outlook's Contacts component to create, import, view, and update records for personal and professional contacts.

Chapter 3, **Organizing and Sharing Outlook Contacts**, reveals Outlook's various sorting tools, as well as how to share your contacts with others (and vice versa).

Chapter 4, **Handling Incoming E-mail**, demonstrates how to set up your Outlook e-mail account to send and receive e-mail messages, as well as how to view, flag, sort, and filter e-mail messages you receive from others.

Chapter 5, **Composing and Sending E-mail Messages**, provides details on replying to and forwarding messages you receive from others, as well as composing new messages. You also discover how to add attachments to and insert photos in your messages, how to use Outlook's proofreading and translation tools, how to change the look of your messages, and more.

Chapter 6, **Text Messaging in Outlook**, explains how to use Outlook to communicate with others on their mobile devices, and how to forward Outlook information to your own mobile device.

Chapter 7, **Using RSS Feeds**, describes how to locate and subscribe to RSS feeds, and how to manage those feeds from within Outlook.

Chapter 8, **Using the Outlook Calendar**, focuses on Outlook's Calendar function, with coverage on switching between day, week, and month views, scheduling appointments, and sharing your calendar with others via the Internet.

Chapter 9, **Using Outlook's Task Component**, covers using Tasks as a to-do list. You discover how to create task entries, sort tasks by various criteria, delegate tasks to others, send status reports for tasks in progress, and more.

Chapter 10, **Using Notes and Journal Entries**, demonstrates how to use Outlook's Notes function to create sticky note-type reminders, as well as how to generate journal entries both manually and automatically to track your time — for example, time spent on a project.

Chapter 11, **Managing Outlook**, illustrates how you can use various Outlook tools and features to organize your contacts, calendar entries, e-mail messages, and tasks — for example, by filing them in folders you create, by categorizing them, by archiving them, and more. You also discover how to protect and troubleshoot Outlook.

Chapter 12, **Customizing Outlook**, covers the myriad ways you can configure Outlook to work for *you*. You learn how to customize the Outlook interface to suit your style of work, change which Outlook component launches at startup, and establish settings for the various Outlook components.

Chapter Organization

Each chapter consists of tasks, all listed in the book's table of contents. A *task* is a set of steps that shows you how to complete a specific computer task.

Each task, usually contained on two facing pages, has an introduction, full-color screen shots, steps that walk you through the task, and a tip. This format allows you to quickly look at a topic of interest and learn it instantly.

Chapters group together three or more tasks with a common theme. A chapter may also contain pages that give you the background information needed to understand the tasks in a chapter.

What You Need to Use This Book

To perform the tasks in this book, you need a personal computer that meets the minimum requirements for any Microsoft Office 2007 product:

- Microsoft Windows XP Service Pack (SP) 2 or later, Microsoft Windows Vista, or Microsoft Windows Server 2003 (or higher) required

- 500 megahertz (MHz) processor or higher; 256 megabyte (MB) RAM or higher

- 2 gigabyte (GB) hard disk space necessary for install; a portion of this disk space will be freed after installation if the original download package is removed from the hard drive

- DVD drive

- Minimum 1024 x 768 monitor resolution

- Broadband Internet connection, 128 kilobits per second (Kbps) or greater, for download and activation of products

Windows Requirements

To get the most out of this book, you need to be running Windows Vista. However, most of the tasks work as written using Windows XP or Windows Server 2003.

Using the Mouse

This book uses the following conventions to describe the actions you perform when using the mouse:

Click

Press your left mouse button once. You generally click your mouse on something to select something on the screen.

Double-click

Press your left mouse button twice. Double-clicking something on the computer screen generally opens whatever item you have double-clicked.

Right-click

Press your right mouse button. When you right-click anything on the computer screen, the program displays a shortcut menu containing commands specific to the selected item.

Click and Drag, and Release the Mouse

Move your mouse pointer and hover it over an item on the screen. Press and hold down the left mouse button. Now, move the mouse to where you want to place the item and then release the button. You use this method to move an item from one area of the computer screen to another.

The Conventions in This Book

A number of typographic and layout styles have been used throughout *Teach Yourself VISUALLY Outlook 2007* to distinguish different types of information.

Bold

Bold type represents the names of commands and options that you interact with. Bold type also indicates text and numbers that you must type into a dialog box or window.

Italics

Italic words introduce a new term and are followed by a definition.

Numbered Steps

You must perform the instructions in numbered steps in order to successfully complete a task and achieve the final results.

Bulleted Text

This text gives you alternative methods, explains various options, or presents what a program will do in response to the numbered steps.

Indented Text

Indented text tells you what the program does in response to you following a numbered step. For example, if you click a certain menu command, a dialog box may appear, or a window may open. Indented text may also tell you what the final result is when you follow a set of numbered steps.

Notes

Notes give additional information. They may describe special conditions that may occur during an operation. They may warn you of a situation that you want to avoid, for example the loss of data. A note may also cross-reference a related area of the book. A cross-reference may guide you to another chapter, or another task within the current chapter.

Icons and Buttons

Icons and buttons are graphical representations within the text. They show you exactly what you need to click to perform a step.

You can easily identify the tips in any task by looking for the TIP icon. Tips offer additional information, including tips, hints, and tricks. You can use the tip information to go beyond what you have learned in the steps.

Exploring Outlook

Whether you are a seasoned user of earlier versions of Outlook or completely new to the program, you will appreciate Microsoft's efforts to streamline the program's interface. By default, the program displays the Mail component, consolidating it with your calendar, upcoming appointments, and tasks on a single screen.

Start and Exit Outlook 2007

Starting Outlook 2007 is a simple matter of selecting the program from the Windows Start menu.

In addition to accessing Outlook from the Start menu, you can also launch it from the desktop, assuming you opted to place a shortcut to the program there.

Start and Exit Outlook 2007

① Click the **Start** button.

The Start menu opens.

② If the Outlook 2007 icon does not appear in the left pane, click **All Programs**.

● Alternatively, if the Outlook 2007 menu item appears in the left pane, click it to start the program.

The All Programs pane opens.

③ Click **Microsoft Office**.

④ Click **Microsoft Office Outlook 2007**.

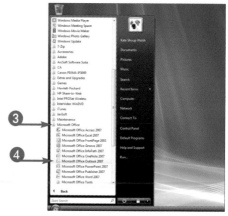

Outlook launches.

5 To exit the program, first click **File**.

6 Click **Exit**.

*Note: Another way to exit Outlook is to click the **Close** button ([×]) in the upper-right corner of the screen.*

Outlook closes.

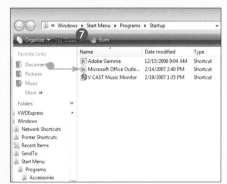

TIP

Can I launch Outlook at start-up?
If you find yourself launching Outlook every time you start Windows, you can configure Windows to launch the program automatically at system start-up. Here's how:

1 Right-click the Outlook program icon in the Start menu.

2 Choose **Copy** from the menu that appears.

3 Click the **Start** button.

4 Click **All Programs**.

5 Right-click the **Startup** folder.

6 Click **Open**.

7 In the window that opens, click **Organize** (in Windows Vista) or **Edit** (in Windows XP).

8 Click **Paste** from the menu that appears.

● An icon for Outlook appears in the Startup folder. The next time you start Windows, Outlook launches automatically.

Outlook 2007 is a personal information-management program designed to help you stay on top of things. Here are a few things Outlook 2007 enables you to do.

Send and Receive E-mails

Using Outlook 2007's Mail component, you can send and receive e-mails. Mail's handy folder system enables you to file your e-mails to keep them organized.

Keep Track of Appointments

Enter upcoming appointments, meetings, and events in Outlook 2007's Calendar component. You can specify whether the entry is recurring, and whether Calendar should remind you of it as it draws near.

Manage Your Contacts

Keep track of your business and personal contacts using Outlook 2007's Contacts component. Available fields include name, e-mail address, phone number(s), mailing address, company name, title, and more.

Maintain a To-Do List

Enter and monitor the tasks, be they large projects or basic chores, pending on your to-do list. You can sort your tasks by many criteria, including category and due date.

Outlook's interface offers easy access to all of the program's components. At start-up, Outlook may launch Outlook Today, which displays upcoming appointments and tasks, as well as how many new messages are in your inbox.

Also visible are the navigation pane, which changes depending on which Outlook component is selected; access to the Calendar, Contacts, and Tasks components; a toolbar, for accessing component-specific tools; and a menu bar for launching component-specific commands.

Menu Bar

Outlook's menu bar offers easy access to component-specific commands. For example, if the Mail component is displayed, the commands available within Outlook's menus pertain specifically to Mail.

Toolbar

The Outlook toolbar enables you to select component-specific tools. For example, if the Calendar component is displayed, the commands available within Outlook's menus pertain specifically to Calendar.

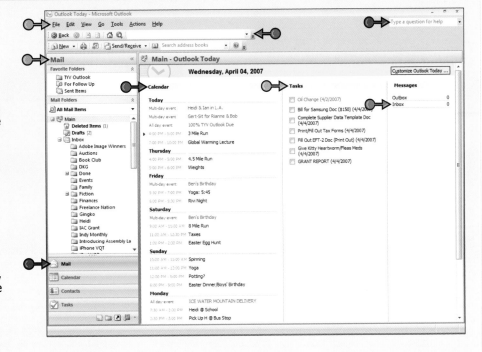

Help Box

You can quickly access Outlook's help information by typing a question or keyword here.

Navigation Pane

The navigation pane changes depending on what Outlook component is selected. Here, the folder list, for filing e-mails, appears. Switching to Mail, Calendar, Contacts, or Tasks changes its contents panel accordingly.

Outlook Component Buttons

To switch from the default Mail component to Calendar, Contacts, or Tasks, click the desired component's button here.

Calendar

Outlook Today lists calendar entries for the next several days.

Tasks

Outlook Today features a task list.

Messages

Outlook Today lists the number of new messages in the inbox.

Understanding the Mail Component

Outlook's Mail component, accessible by clicking the Mail component button, enables you to view, respond to, forward, and compose new e-mails.

You can create folders for organizing the e-mails you send and receive.
Mail-specific tools and commands appear in the toolbar and menu bar.

Menu Bar

The Mail menu bar enables you to create, print, edit, reply to, and categorize messages; switch to other Outlook components; set follow-up parameters; and more.

Toolbar

Use the buttons in the Mail toolbar as an alternative way to execute many of the Mail-specific commands found in the menu bar.

Folder List

Mail's folder list includes several default folders, including Deleted Items, Drafts, Inbox, Junk E-mail, Outbox, and Sent Items. You can create additional, custom folders for organizing and storing your messages.

Mail Component Button

If the Mail component is not currently displayed, click the Mail component button to display it.

Message List

By default, Mail displays a list of the messages in your Inbox folders, although the message list can display messages in other folders if you click the desired folder in the folder list.

Instant Search Box

You can quickly locate e-mails, appointments, and other Outlook entries by typing relevant keywords into the Instant Search box.

Reading Pane

To read a message in your message list, click it; the message text appears in the reading pane.

To-Do Bar

If you are working in Mail, Contacts, or Tasks, Outlook displays the To-Do bar. It features a date navigator, upcoming appointments, and your task list.

When you open an e-mail message you receive from someone else, reply to a message, or create a new message, Outlook launches a message window. Note that the options available in the message window differ depending on what type of message the window contains.

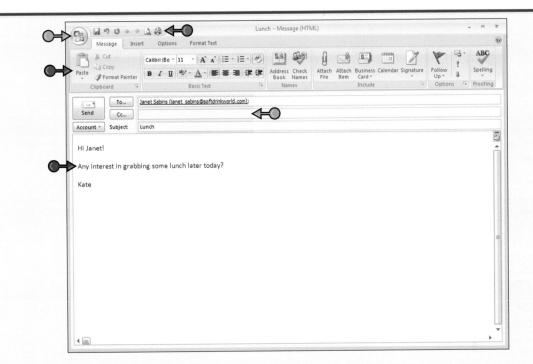

Office Button

This button provides access to oft-used commands, such as Save, Delete, Print, and more.

Quick Access Toolbar

Like the Office button, the Quick Access toolbar offers access to frequently used commands. You can customize this toolbar, removing commands that appear there by default and adding others you use more often.

Ribbon

In lieu of the traditional menus and toolbars, message windows feature the *Ribbon* — that is, a tabbed area in which commands are organized in logical groups. The precise tabs and commands present on the Ribbon differ depending on what type of window is open.

Sender/Recipient/Subject

Information about the sender, recipient, and subject of the message can be entered or located here.

Message Body

Read or enter the message contents here.

Understanding the Calendar Component

Outlook's Calendar component, accessible by clicking the Calendar component button, allows you to enter and view appointments by day (the default), by week, or by month.

If you choose to view appointments by day or week, a list of tasks due on the selected date(s) also appears. Calendar-specific tools and commands appear in the toolbar and menu bar.

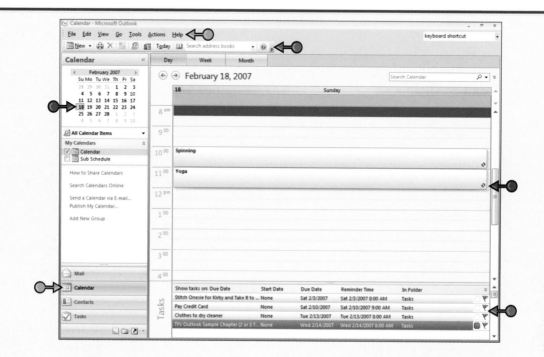

Menu Bar

The Calendar menu bar enables you to create, print, edit, and categorize appointments, events, and meetings; switch to other Calendar views as well as to other Outlook components; and more.

Toolbar

Use the buttons in the Calendar toolbar as an alternative way to execute many of the Calendar-specific commands found in the menu bar.

Date Navigator

Use this small month long calendar to quickly navigate within the current month or to a different month altogether. Available under the date navigator

are links for sharing, searching, sending, and publishing calendars.

Calendar Component Button

If the Calendar component is not currently displayed, click the Calendar component button to display it.

Calendar

By default, Calendar displays appointments by day, but week and month views are also available.

Tasks Pane

If you opt to view your appointments by day or week, tasks due on the visible day appear here.

When you open a calendar entry, whether it is for an appointment, an event, or a meeting, Outlook launches a calendar window. (Note that the options available in the calendar window differ slightly depending on what type of calendar entry the window contains.)

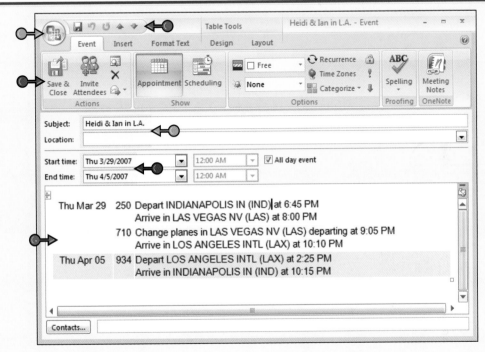

Office Button

This button provides access to oft-used commands, such as Save, Delete, Print, and more.

Quick Access Toolbar

Like the Office button, the Quick Access toolbar offers access to frequently used commands. You can customize this toolbar, removing commands that appear there by default and adding others you use more often.

Ribbon

In lieu of the traditional menus and toolbars, message windows feature the *Ribbon* — that is, a tabbed area in which commands are organized in logical groups.

Subject/Location

Information about the subject and location of the calendar entry can be entered or located here.

Start Time/End Time

Information about the start date and time and end date and time can be entered or located here.

Notes

Read or enter notes about the calendar entry.

Understanding the Contacts Component

Outlook's Contacts component, accessible from the Contacts component button, allows you to enter and view contacts.

Contacts can be sorted alphabetically by category, by company, or by location. You can specify how much information should appear for each contact in the list. You can view additional information about a contact by opening it.

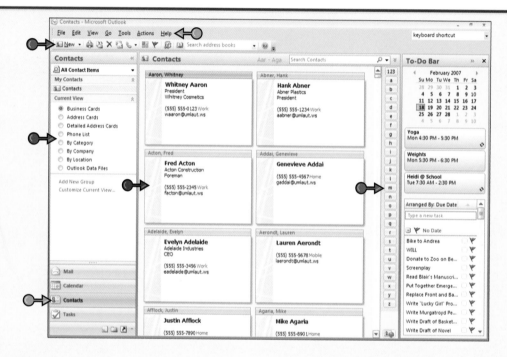

Menu Bar

The Contacts menu bar enables you to create, print, edit, share, and categorize contacts; switch to other Outlook components; and more.

Toolbar

Use the buttons in the Contacts toolbar as an alternative way to execute many of the Contacts-specific commands found in the menu bar.

View Options

Choose how you want to view your contacts: as business cards, as detailed address cards, by category, and so on.

Contacts Component Button

If the Contacts component is not currently displayed, click the Contacts component button to display it.

Contacts List

By default, Contacts displays a list of your contacts in Business Card form.

Alphabetized "Thumb Tabs"

To jump to contacts whose names start with a different letter, click the appropriate letter here.

When you open a contact entry, Outlook launches a contact window. This window contains fields for entering or reviewing information about a contact, such as Full Name, Job Title, E-mail, and so on.

Office Button

This button provides access to oft-used commands, such as Save, Delete, Print, and more.

Quick Access Toolbar

Like the Office button, the Quick Access toolbar offers access to frequently used commands. You can customize this toolbar, removing commands that appear there by default and adding others you use more often.

Ribbon

In lieu of the traditional menus and toolbars, message windows feature the *Ribbon* — that is, a tabbed area in which commands are organized in logical groups.

Name

The contact's name, company, and job title can be entered or located here.

Internet

The contact's e-mail address, Web page address, and IM address can be entered or located here.

Phone Numbers

The contact's phone numbers can be entered or located here.

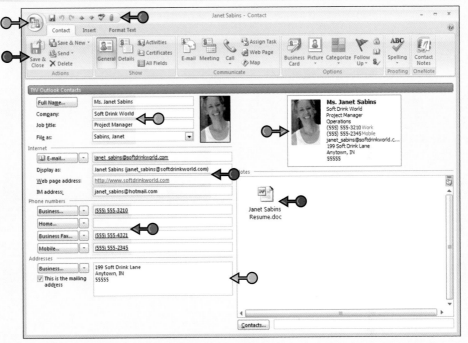

Addresses

The contact's addresses can be entered or located here.

Business Card

An electronic "business card" containing information you enter about the contact appears here.

Notes

Read or enter notes about the contact.

Understanding the Tasks Component

Outlook's Tasks component, accessible by clicking the Tasks component button, allows you to keep track of your tasks — that is, chores you need to complete, errands you need to run, and other items you would normally jot down in a to-do list.

Tasks can be sorted alphabetically, by category, by due date, and more.

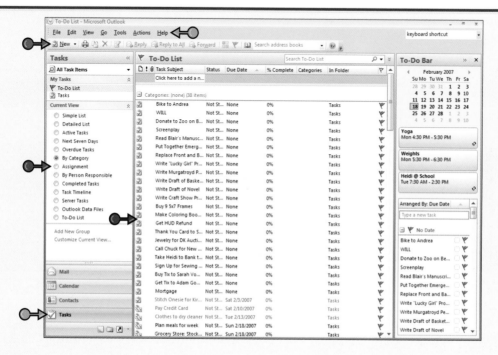

Menu Bar

The Tasks menu bar enables you to create, print, edit, share, and categorize tasks; switch to other Outlook components; and more.

Toolbar

Use the buttons in the Tasks toolbar as an alternative way to execute many of the Tasks-specific commands found in the menu bar.

View Options

Choose how you want to view your tasks: as a simple list, as a detailed list, by category, by due date, and so on.

Tasks Component Button

If the Tasks component is not currently displayed, click the Tasks component button to display it.

Tasks List

Tasks displays a list of the tasks in your list, sorted and presented according to the settings you establish.

When you open a task entry, Outlook launches a task window. This window contains fields for entering or reviewing information about the task, such as its due date, priority, owner, notes, and so on.

Office Button
This button provides access to oft-used commands, such as Save, Delete, Print, and more.

Quick Access Toolbar
Like the Office button, the Quick Access toolbar offers access to frequently used commands. You can customize this toolbar, removing commands that appear there by default and adding others you use more often.

Ribbon
In lieu of the traditional menus and toolbars, message windows feature the *Ribbon* — that is, a tabbed area in which commands are organized in logical groups.

Subject
The task's subject, or description, can be entered or located here.

Start Date/Due Date
The task's start date and due date can be entered or located here.

Status/Priority/Percentage Complete
The task's status, priority, and percentage complete can be entered or located here.

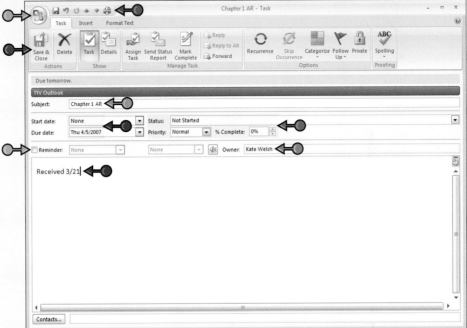

Reminder
The contact's reminder status can be entered or located here.

Owner
The task's owner can be entered or located here.

Notes
Read or enter notes about the task here.

Manage Daily Priorities with the To-Do Bar

Outlook's To-Do bar, located on the far-right side of the Outlook interface, enables you to see at a glance a monthly calendar, upcoming appointments entered into the Calendar component, and pending tasks.

The To-Do bar is visible on the screen when the Mail, Contacts, or Tasks Outlook component is active, but not the Calendar.

Manage Daily Priorities with the To-Do Bar

SWITCH DAYS

① Click a date in the To-Do bar's date navigator.

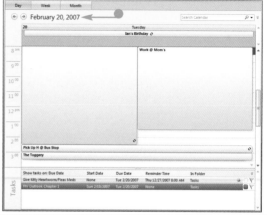

● Outlook switches to the Calendar component to display the appointments for the date you clicked.

VIEW AN APPOINTMENT

① With the Mail, Contacts, or Tasks component active, double-click an appointment listed in the To-Do bar.

● Outlook opens the appointment in its own window, where you can edit it as needed.

ADD A TASK

① To add a new task to the list, type a name for it and press Enter.

The task is added to the list.

● To sort the tasks in the To-Do bar by a different criterion, click the name of the current criterion. A list of criteria appears; click the criterion by which you want to sort your tasks.

TIP

Can I resize the To-Do bar?

If you find that the To-Do bar is too narrow, making it difficult to see the names of the tasks in your Tasks list, resize the To-Do bar. To do so, place your mouse pointer over the left edge of the bar. Your cursor changes to a vertical bar with arrows pointing from either side (✛); click and drag to the left to widen the To-Do bar. To make the To-Do bar narrow again, repeat these steps, but drag to the right.

Regardless of which Outlook component you are using, you can search for Outlook items such as messages, contacts, appointments, and so on.

Note that although you can use the Instant Search feature in all of Outlook's components, this task focuses on searching for e-mail messages.

Perform an Instant Search

① With the Outlook Mail component displayed, click the folder in which you think the message is located.

② Type a keyword or phrase in the Instant Search box.

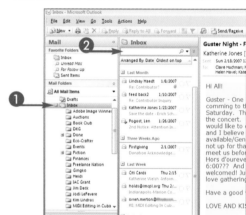

● As you type, Outlook displays a list of the messages containing the string of letters you typed.

③ To narrow your search, type more characters in the Instant Search box.

④ To widen your search to include all Mail folders (rather than just the folder you selected in Step ①), click the **Try Searching Again in All Mail Items** link.

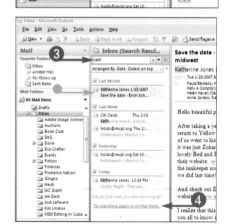

⑤ To add more search criteria, click the **Expand the Query Builder** arrow ().

● Outlook displays the Query Builder, which contains several blank fields for typing additional criteria.

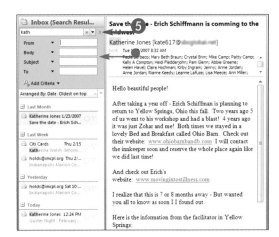

⑥ Type additional criteria as needed in the From, Body, Subject, and/or To fields.

● Outlook displays a list of messages that match your criteria.

● To add more criteria to the Query Builder, click the **Add Criteria** button and choose the criterion you want to add. Remove a criterion by clicking the down arrow () next to the Add Criteria button and choosing **Remove** from the drop-down list that opens.

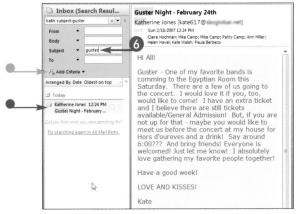

TIP

Can I recycle a recent search?
If you recently searched for the message you need to find, you can simply recycle that earlier search rather than building a new one. To do so, click the **Instant Search** and choose **Recent Searches**. Outlook displays a list of your ten most recent searches; select the one you want to recycle.

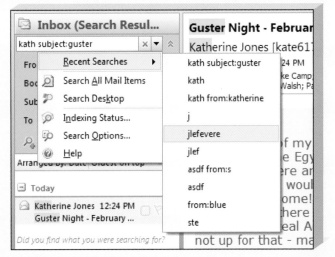

Get Help

You can find out more about Outlook 2007, learn how to perform a task, or troubleshoot problems by using the program's Help system.

Most of the Help system is arranged into various topics, such as What's New, E-mail, Calendar and Scheduling, Contacts, Tasks, and so on. Each topic offers a number of subtopics, and each subtopic contains a collection of related tasks, articles, tutorials, and other items.

Get Help

① Click **Help**.

The Help menu opens.

② Click **Microsoft Office Outlook Help**.

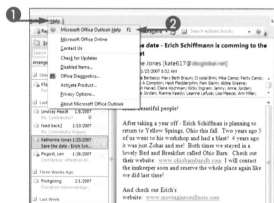

The Help window opens.

③ Click a topic.

● The Help window reveals a list of
subtopics.

Clicking a subtopic next to a 📵 icon
reveals an article or series of steps for
accomplishing a task.

Clicking a subtopic next to a 🖥 icon
launches an interactive training session.

④ Click a subtopic (here, one with a
question-mark icon).

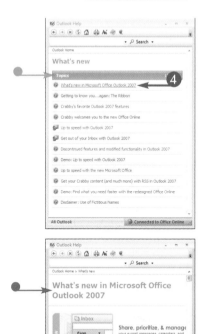

● The help information is displayed.

Are there other help options?
Another way to launch Outlook's Help window is to click the
Help button (📵) on the toolbar. An even better option is to type
a keyword or phrase in the Help box in the upper-right corner
of the Outlook screen (above the To-Do bar); when you press
Enter, the Help window opens, with links displayed to information
about the word or phrase you typed.

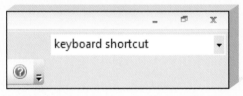

CHAPTER 2

Creating and Using Outlook Contacts

You can keep track of your business and personal contacts using Outlook 2007's Contacts component. You specify how much information appears for each of your contacts; available fields include name, e-mail, phone number(s), mailing address, company name, title, and more. Contacts can be sorted alphabetically, by category, by company, or by location.

Create a Contact

Outlook 2007's Contacts component stores information about people — phone numbers, fax numbers, e-mail addresses, postal addresses, Web site addresses, personal information, notes, even photos.

You are not required to enter all this information for a contact. To create a contact entry, only a name is required. Adding more information, however, better enables you to keep track of your contacts.

Create a Contact

① If Contacts is not currently open, click the **Contacts** button in the navigation pane.

Outlook switches to Contacts.

② Click the **New** button.

A Contact window opens.

③ Type your contact's name, and, optionally, his or her company name and job title.

④ Type your contact's e-mail address.

● You can enter as many as three e-mail addresses for a contact. To enter the second or third addresses, click ⬛ next to the E-mail field, choose **E-mail 2** or **E-mail 3**, and type the additional address.

⑤ In the Display As box, type the contact's name as you want it to appear in the To line of an e-mail message.

⑥ If applicable, type your contact's Web page address.

⑦ If applicable, type your contact's IM address.

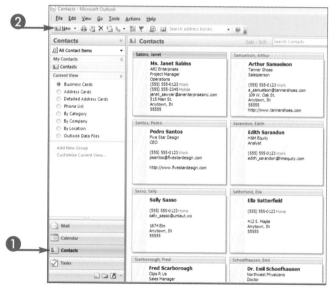

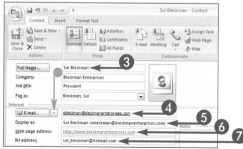

⑧ Type your contact's business, home, fax, and mobile phone numbers.

⑨ Type your contact's mailing address.

● If the address you want to type is the contact's home address rather than a business address, click ▾ next to Business and choose **Home** from the list that appears.

● Click the **This is the Mailing Address** check box (☐ changes to ☑) to establish which address should be used during a mail-merge operation.

⑩ Type any notes about your contact.

⑪ Click the **Details** button.

The Details window opens.

⑫ Type the contact's department, office, and profession.

⑬ Type the name of the contact's manager and assistant.

⑭ Type personal information about the contact, such as his or her nickname and the name of the contact's spouse.

⑮ Click **Save & Close**.

The contact is added to Outlook.

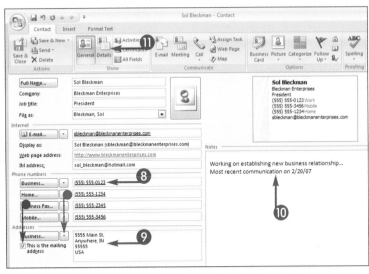

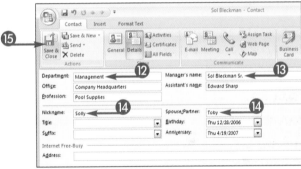

TIPS

Can I duplicate company information?

If you need to enter a new contact who works in the same company as another contact you have entered, click the existing contact to select it, click **Actions**, and then click **New Contact from Same Company**. A Contact window opens, with the company information already filled in.

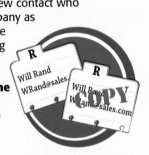

How do I add special dates?

To enter a contact's birthday or anniversary, click the **Business** or **Anniversary** ▾ and click the applicable date from the date navigator that appears. When you add a birthday or anniversary in Contacts, it is also saved in Calendar.

Import Contacts

You can import contacts from another contacts-management program into Outlook's Contacts. This saves you the time it takes to retype all of your contacts from the other program.

Note that if you upgraded from an earlier edition of Outlook to Outlook 2007, your contacts are imported automatically.

Import Contacts

① If Contacts is not currently open, click the **Contacts** button in the navigation pane.

Outlook switches to Contacts.

② Click **File**.

③ Click **Import and Export**.

Note: *Before you can import your contacts, you may first need to export your contacts from the original contacts-management program. When you do, pay attention to what type of file the export operation creates, as well as where you save the exported file. For more information, refer to that program's help information.*

● The Import and Export Wizard opens.

④ Click **Import from Another Program or File**.

⑤ Click **Next**.

⑥ In the Import a File page, click the type of file you want to import.

This example selects a comma-separated value file.

⑦ Click **Next**.

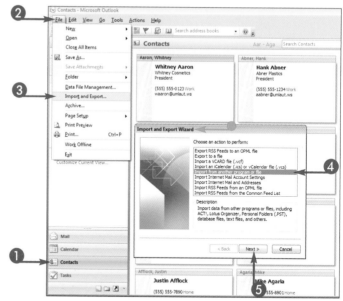

● Outlook locates a file of the type you selected.

● If the file Outlook detects is not the one you want to import, click the **Browse** button and locate the correct file.

8 Click an option for how you want Outlook to handle duplicate entries (○ changes to ◉).

9 Click **Next**.

● By default, Outlook saves the imported file in the Contacts folder.

10 Click **Next**.

11 Click **Finish**.

Outlook imports the contacts.

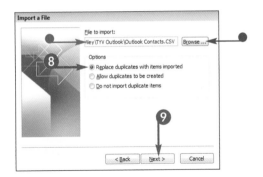

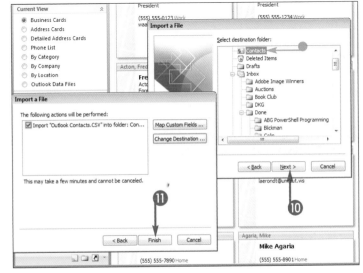

TIPS

How do I obtain an imported file?

If the file you want to import lives on another computer, and if that computer is not accessible to you via a network, you need to copy the file onto a CD or some other type of removable media and then transfer it to your system in an easy-to-remember location.

Can I mark contacts as private?

To prevent others from viewing the details of a particular contact, you can lock it. To do so, click the **Private** button (🔒) in the Contact tab's Options group.

View a
Contact

Viewing contact information in Outlook 2007 could not be simpler. You just locate the desired entry in Contacts and double-click it to view it.

① If Contacts is not currently open, click the **Contacts** button in the navigation pane.

Outlook switches to Contacts.

② Click the first letter of the contact's last name.

● Outlook jumps to the contacts that start with the selected letter.

③ If necessary, scroll up or down to locate the contact.

● An even quicker way to locate a contact is to search for it by typing the contact's name in the Search Contacts field. As you type, Contacts automatically locates entries that match.

④ To see more information about the contact, double-click it.

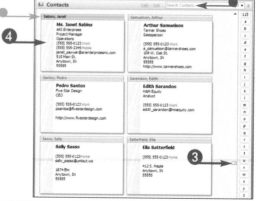

● The contact opens in its own window.

5 View the contact information.

6 To see more information about the contact, click **Details**.

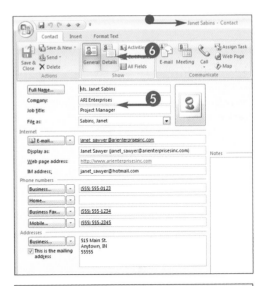

● The Details screen opens.

7 View more details about the contact.

8 To close the contact window, click its **Close** button ([×]).

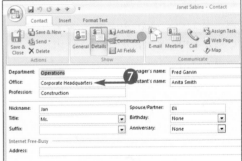

Can I call a contact?

If your computer is set up for telephony, you can use it to phone a contact directly from within Outlook. To do so, open the record for the contact you want to call, click **Call** in the Contact tab's Communicate group, select which of the contact's phone numbers you want to dial in the New Call dialog box, and click **Start Call**.

How do I verify a contact's info?

To ensure that a contact's name and e-mail address have been typed correctly, click the **Check Names** button ([✓]) in the Contact tab's Options group.

Update a Contact

Inevitably, people move, change jobs, get married (or divorced), or otherwise alter their circumstances — meaning you need to update their information in Contacts to keep up. Fortunately, Contacts makes it easy to edit contact information.

Update a Contact

① If Contacts is not currently open, click the **Contacts** button in the navigation pane.

Outlook switches to Contacts.

② Click the first letter of the contact's last name.

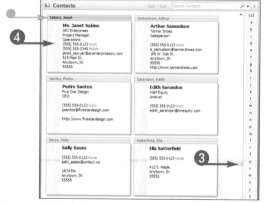

● Outlook jumps to the contacts that start with the selected letter.

③ If necessary, scroll up or down to locate the contact.

④ Double-click the contact you want to edit.

● The contact record opens in its own window.

⑤ Double-click a field that needs updating and type over the existing text with the new, correct information. Repeat as needed until all necessary fields are changed.

● Information in the Details screen can also be edited.

⑥ When you finish updating the necessary fields, click **Save & Close**.

● The contact's information is updated.

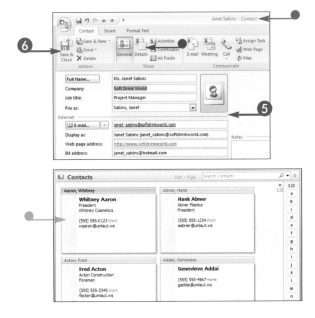

TIP

Is there another way to update a contact?

Another way to update a contact is via the All Fields page, which displays all the information about a contact in a table. (Because of space constraints, some fields that are visible in the All Fields page may not appear in the contact record.) Follow these steps:

① Open the contact you want to edit.

② In the Contact tab's Show group, click the **All Fields** button.

③ Click the **Select From** ▾ and choose the type of information you want to add or change.

④ In the Name column, locate the field whose value you want to change.

⑤ Type the desired value for the field in the Value column.

⑥ Click **Save & Close** to update the contact record.

In addition to changing existing fields, you can also add new fields to the contact record. For more information, see Outlook's help files.

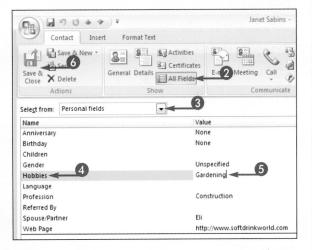

Add a Picture to a Contact

For many people, putting a face to a name can be difficult. To help, Outlook enables you to attach a photograph to a contact record.

When you add a picture to a contact, anytime you receive a message from that person, his or her picture appears in the message header.

Add a Picture to a Contact

1 If Contacts is not currently open, click the **Contacts** button in the navigation pane.

Outlook switches to Contacts.

2 Locate the contact to which you want to attach a picture and double-click it to open it.

● The contact record opens in its own window.

3 Click the **Add Contact Picture** button.

The Add Contact Picture dialog box appears.

④ Locate the picture you want to add to the contact record and click it to select it.

● If the Add Contact Picture dialog box displays your image files in Details view, preventing you from seeing the images themselves, click **Views** and click **Medium Icons**, **Large Icons**, or **Extra Large Icons**.

⑤ Click the **OK** button.

● The picture is added to the contact record.

⑥ Click **Save & Close**.

The contact is updated to include the picture you added.

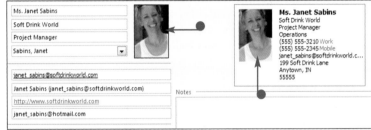

Can I change or remove the picture?

To change a picture associated with a contact record, open the record, right-click the picture, and choose **Change Picture** (●). The Change Contact Picture dialog box appears. Locate the picture you want to use instead, click it to select it, and click **Open**. In the contact window, click **Save & Close**. To remove a picture from a contact record, open the record, right-click the picture, and choose **Remove Picture**.

You may find it necessary to attach a file to a contact record. For example, suppose one of your contacts e-mails you her résumé. You can attach that résumé to her contact record for easy access.

Attach a File to a Contact

① If Contacts is not currently open, click the **Contacts** button in the navigation pane.

Outlook switches to Contacts.

② Locate the contact to which you want to attach a file and double-click it to open it.

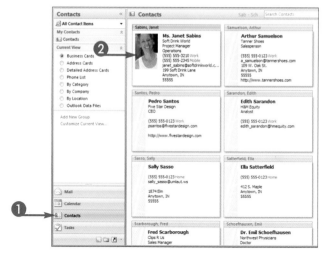

● The contact record opens in its own window.

③ Click the **Insert** tab.

④ In the Include group, click **Attach File**.

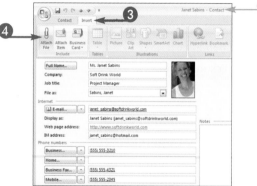

The Insert File dialog box appears.

5 Locate the file you want to attach to the contact record and click it to select it.

6 Click the **Insert** button.

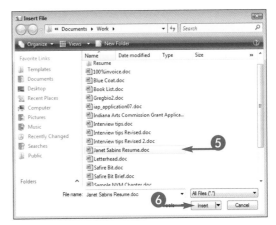

An icon representing the file is placed in the Notes section of the contact record.

7 Click the **Contact** tab.

8 Click **Save & Close**.

The contact is updated to include the file you added.

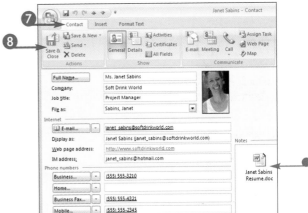

TIP

Can I attach Outlook items to a contact?

In addition to attaching files to a contact, you can also attach an Outlook item, such as an e-mail message, an appointment, or a task. To do so, follow these steps:

1 Open the desired contact.

2 Click the **Insert** tab.

3 Click **Attach Item**.

4 In the Insert Item dialog box, locate the item you want to attach, and click it to select it.

5 Click **OK**.

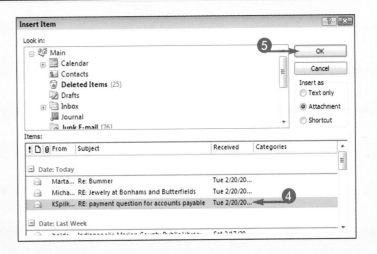

Locate an Address with Contacts Maps

If you plan to visit someone listed in Contacts, and if that person's contact record includes an address, you can use the Contacts map feature.

In addition to enabling you to view a map pinpointing the contact's location, you can also obtain directions from your location to your destination. Note that in order to use Contact's mapping function, you must be online.

Locate an Address with Contacts Maps

① With the window for the contact whose location you want to map open in Outlook, click ▾ under Addresses and choose **Home**, **Business**, or **Other** to select the address you need.

② In the Contact tab's Communicate group, click the **Map** button.

● A Windows Live Web page opens, pinpointing the contact's location.

③ To obtain directions from your current location to the contact's, place your cursor over the address link.

④ Click the **Drive To** link from the list of options that appears.

● The contact's address is added to the End field in the Driving Directions panel.

⑤ Type your starting address in the Start field.

⑥ Click either the **Shortest Time** or **Shortest Distance** option (◎ changes to ◉).

⑦ Click **Get Directions**.

● The map changes to show your route.

Note: *You may need to click the* ***Close*** *button (✖) in the Scratch Pad to close it in order to see the full route.*

⑧ To print the directions, click the **Print** ▾ in the Driving Directions pane and specify whether you want to print the map of the route, text directions, or both.

⑨ To send the directions to your mobile device or via e-mail click the **Send** ▾, select the appropriate option, and follow the on-screen prompts.

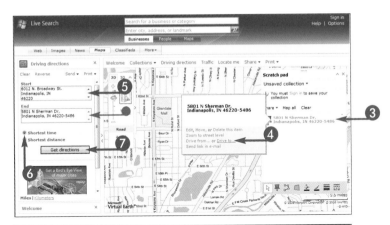

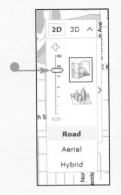

(TIPS)

How do I zoom in?
You can easily zoom into the map in order to see it in more detail. To do so, click and drag the Zoom slider (●) provided on the page.

How do I switch to Aerial view?
By default, the map is displayed in Road view, like a typical map. You can, however, click **Aerial** in the Zoom slider to switch to Aerial view, which is a satellite image of the location. In addition, you can click **Hybrid** in the Zoom slider to switch to Hybrid view, which combines elements of the Road and Aerial views.

Create an Electronic Business Card

Just as you likely exchange paper-based business cards with others, you can also exchange business cards created with Contacts. You can then send your business cards to others via e-mail, either as an attachment or as part of your e-mail message's signature. (You learn how to send an electronic business card in Chapter 3.)

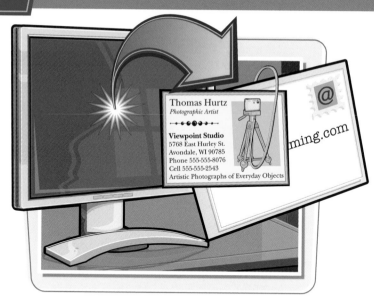

Create an Electronic Business Card

1 If Contacts is not currently open, click the **Contacts** button in the navigation pane.

Outlook switches to Contacts.

2 Click the **New** button.

● If you have already typed your own contact information into Outlook, simply open your contact entry rather than create a new one.

3 Type your contact information.

4 In the Options group of the Contact tab, click **Business Card**.

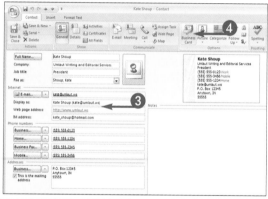

The Edit Business Card dialog box appears.

⑤ Click the **Layout** 🔽.

⑥ Specify where you want the image on the electronic business card to appear.

In this example, Image Left is selected.

⑦ Click the **Background** button (🖼️).

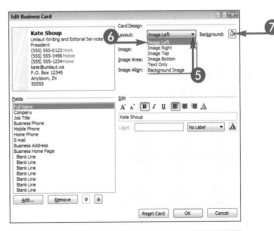

● The Color dialog box appears.

⑧ Choose a background color for the electronic business card.

● If none of the available colors suits you, you can click **Define Custom Colors**, then click a color in the large square that appears, fine-tune your selection in the strip to the right, and click **Add to Custom Colors**. Then select the color under Custom Colors on the left side of the window.

⑨ Click **OK**.

⑩ To change the image displayed, click the **Change** button in the Edit Business Card dialog box.

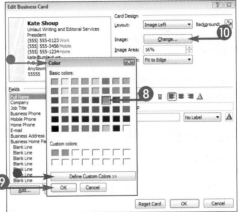

Can I view other contacts as electronic business cards?

In addition to creating an electronic business card that contains your contact information to share with others, you can also configure Outlook to display the contacts it stores in electronic business card form, much the way Rolodexes of old could be made to store paper-based business cards. To view your contact entries as electronic business cards, click the **Business Cards** option (⚪ changes to ⚫) in the navigation pane under Current View.

continued

In addition to including vital information such as your name, phone number, e-mail address, and so on, your electronic business card can also include a photo and/or a logo. You can also customize the design of your electronic business card.

Create an Electronic Business Card *(continued)*

The Add Card Picture dialog box appears.

⑪ Locate the image you want to include on your electronic business card and click it to select it.

Note: *You need not use a photograph on the card; an image file containing your company's logo, for example, also works.*

⑫ Click **OK**.

⑬ Click the spin arrow (⬍) to adjust the size of the image on the card.

⑭ Click the **Image Align** ⬇ and specify how the image should be aligned.

⑮ To add a field to the card, click **Add** and choose the desired field.

Business Home Page is selected in this example.

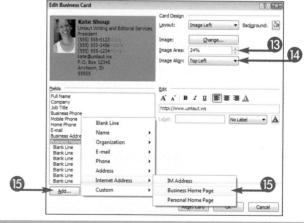

16 To omit a field — for example, Home Phone — click it in the list and click Remove.

17 To change the order of the fields, click a field you want to move, and then click either ⬆ or ⬇.

18 To adjust a field's font or alignment, click the field in the list and then click any of the following:

Click **A** or **A** to increase or decrease font size, respectively.

Click **B**, **I**, and/or **U** to make the text bold, italic, or underlined, respectively.

Click ▤, ▤, or ▤ to left-align, center-align, or right-align the text, respectively.

Click **A** to change the font color. This launches the Color dialog box; choose the font color the same way you did the background color.

19 Click **OK**.

● The business card is saved in your contact record.

20 Click **Save & Close**.

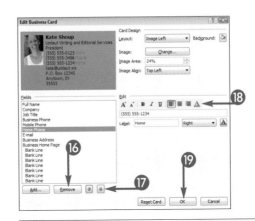

 TIP

Can I label a field?
Rather than having a separate field for, say, your job title, you might add that information as a label to the Full Name field. To do so, in the Label section of the Edit Business Card dialog box, click ▾ to specify whether the label should appear to the left or the right of the existing text. Then type the label and choose the desired font color (**A**).

Organizing and Sharing Outlook Contacts

Simply being able to enter contacts into Outlook is not helpful if you cannot find the one you need, when you need it. Fortunately, Outlook makes it easy to sort and find your contacts. Outlook also makes it easy to share your contacts with others.

Change Views

By default, contacts are displayed in Business Cards view. To see more entries at once, you can switch to Address Cards view. A third view, Detailed Address Cards, displays more information about each contact than Address Cards view, with each entry consuming less screen space than in Business Cards view. Finally, you can view your contacts as a phone list.

Change Views

① If Contacts is not currently open, click the **Contacts** button in the navigation pane.

● Outlook switches to Contacts, in Business Cards view.

② Under Current View in the navigation pane, click the **Address Cards** option (◎ changes to ⦿).

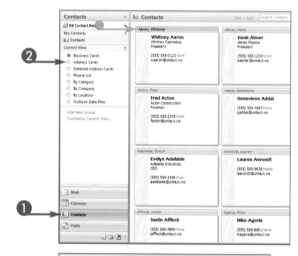

● Outlook switches to Address Cards view.

③ Click the **Detailed Address Cards** option (◎ changes to ⦿).

- Outlook switches to Detailed Address Cards view.

④ Click the **Phone List** option (◎ changes to ◉).

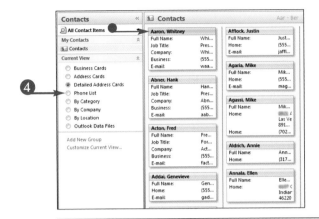

- Outlook switches to Phone List view.

TIPS

Are there other ways to switch views?

In addition to selecting the options in the Contacts navigation pane to switch views, you can also use Outlook's View menu. Simply click **View**, **Current View**, and then select the view you want. You might opt for this approach if, for example, you have hidden the navigation pane to increase the space available for other parts of the Outlook screen.

Can I create a custom view?

You can easily create a custom view, either using an existing standard view as your base or starting from scratch. To create a new view, click **View**, **Current View**, and then **Customize Current View** to base the new view on an existing one or click **View**, **Current View**, and then **Define Views** to create a new view from scratch, and select the desired options in the dialog box that appears (●). For guidance, see Outlook's help system.

Sort
Contacts

Your contacts can be sorted in any number of ways: by name (the default), by category, by company, or even by location. You can also create custom sort parameters, as you learn in the next task.

You can learn how to apply a category to a contact — as well as to other Outlook items — in Chapter 11.

Sort Contacts

① If Contacts is not currently open, click the **Contacts** button in the navigation pane.

● Outlook switches to Contacts, in Business Card view.

② Under Current View in the navigation pane, click the **By Category** option (⦾ changes to ⦿).

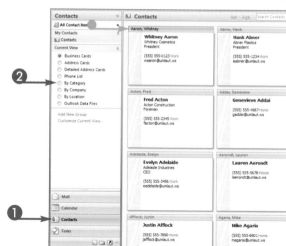

● Outlook sorts your contacts by category.

③ Click the **By Company** option (⦾ changes to ⦿).

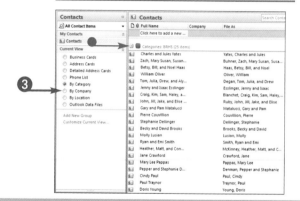

● Outlook sorts your contacts by company.

④ Click the **By Location** option
(◎ changes to ◉).

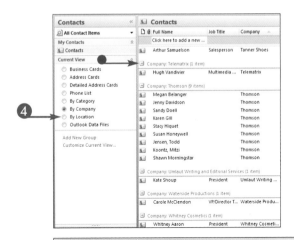

● Outlook sorts your contacts by location.

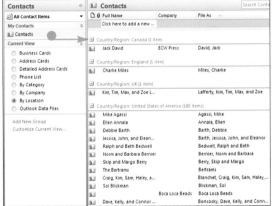

 TIPS

Can I sort contacts in other views?
In Business Cards, Address Cards, and Detailed Address Cards views, contacts are sorted alphabetically only. In Phone List view, however, contacts can be sorted by any number of fields, such as Full Name, Company, Category, and more. Simply click the heading containing the field by which you want to sort your contacts (●).

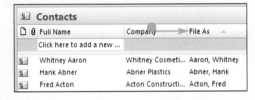

Can I change how my contacts list looks?
If you do not care for the font used in Contacts by default, you can change it, as well as other graphics-oriented settings such as how the grid looks. To do so, click **View**, **Current View**, and then **Customize Current View**. In the Customize View dialog box that appears, click the **Other Settings** button and adjust the settings as desired in the Other Settings dialog box.

Customize the Sort Operation

Suppose you sort your contacts by category, but you want to refine the operation by sorting the entries within each category. For example, you might want to display all contacts in the Work category by company. You might then want to sort those entries alphabetically by last name. Fortunately, Outlook makes it easy to customize the sort operation.

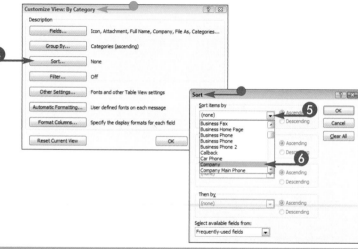

Customize the Sort Operation

① After sorting your contacts by category (as shown here), by company, or by location, click **View**.

② Click **Current View**.

③ Click **Customize Current View**.

● The Customize View dialog box appears.

④ Click the **Sort** button.

● The Sort dialog box appears.

⑤ Click the **Sort Items By** 🔽.

⑥ Choose the parameter by which you want to sort.

This example shows **Company** as the selected parameter.

Note: You may need to drag the scroll bar in the drop-down list to locate the desired field.

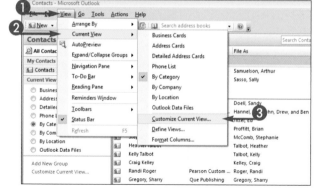

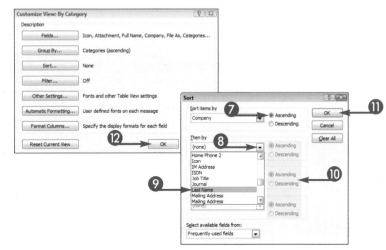

7 If you want the companies in your list to appear from A to Z, select the **Ascending** option; to display them from Z to A, select the **Descending** option.

8 To add a second sort parameter, click the **Then By** ▾.

9 Choose the second parameter by which you want to sort.

Last Name is selected in this example.

10 Repeat Step **7** to indicate whether the names should be listed in ascending or descending order.

Note: If desired, you can add as many as four parameters, although this task stops at two.

11 Click **OK** to close the Sort dialog box.

12 Click **OK** to close the Customize View dialog box.

● Your contacts are sorted accordingly.

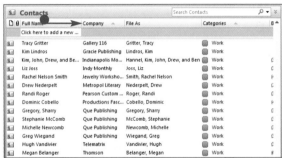

 TIPS

How can I undo a custom sort?

To undo a custom sort, click **View**, **Arrange By**, and then **Custom**. In the Customize View dialog box that appears, click **Sort**. In the Sort dialog box, open the Sort Items By list and click **None** (●). Finally, click **OK** in the Sort and Customize View dialog boxes.

Are there other ways to view contacts?

One way to quickly view contact information is to work with the reading pane visible. That way, if you click a contact in the list, you instantly see the contact record in its own pane on the screen. To open the pane, click the **Other Settings** button in the Customize View dialog box; then, in the Other Settings dialog box, click either the **Right** or **Bottom** option under the reading pane. Finally, click **OK** in the Other Settings and Customize View dialog boxes.

Resolve Duplicate Contacts

If you create a new contact, but Outlook already contains an entry with the same name or e-mail address, the program notifies you that the new entry is a duplicate.

You can add the duplicate entry as a new contact or combine the information you typed in the duplicate contact with what is in the existing one, as shown here.

Resolve Duplicate Contacts

① If Contacts is not currently open, click the **Contacts** button in the navigation pane.

Outlook switches to Contacts.

② Click **New**.

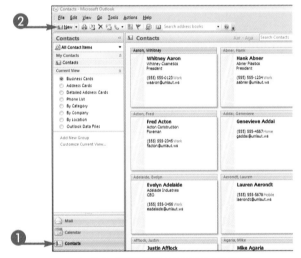

A blank Contact window opens.

③ Type the necessary contact information.

Note: For more information about creating a new contact, see Chapter 2.

④ Click **Save & Close**.

If the contact is a duplicate, the Duplicate Contact Detected dialog box appears.

5 Click the **Update Information of Selected Contact** option (⊙ changes to ⊙).

● The existing contact appears in the field below the option button.

Note: *If more than one existing contact matches the new one, each will be listed here; make sure the contact that is selected is indeed the one you want to update.*

● A preview of the updated contact appears here.

● View what changes will be made to the existing contact here.

6 Click **Update**.

● Outlook updates the contact.

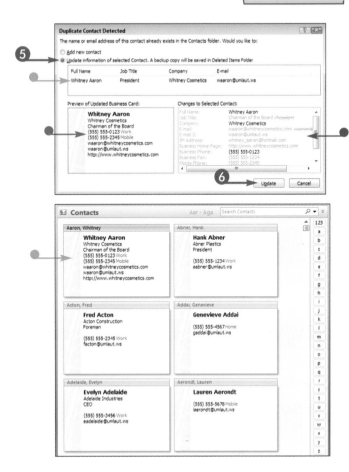

How do I add the contact as a duplicate?

If you want to add the duplicate as a new contact — for example, if you know two individuals who share the same name — click the **Add New Contact** option (⊙ changes to ⊙) and then click the **Add** button in the lower-right corner of the Duplicate Contact Detected dialog box.

How do I delete an existing duplicate?

Especially if you import contacts into Outlook, you may wind up with some unwanted duplicate entries — new records that contain the same name or e-mail address as existing records. The best way to detect these duplicates is to switch to Phone List view and quickly scan for repeats. If you find one, right-click it and choose **Delete** from the menu that appears.

Export Contacts

In addition to importing contacts into Outlook, you can export your Outlook contacts. The exported contacts file can then be imported by another contacts-management program.

When you export contacts, you typically do so as a CSV (short for comma-separated values) file, a generic file format used for exporting and importing information to and from databases, spreadsheets, and contacts-management programs.

Export Contacts

① If Contacts is not currently open, click the **Contacts** button in the navigation pane.

Outlook switches to Contacts.

② Click **File**.

③ Click **Import and Export**.

● The Import and Export Wizard starts.

④ Click **Export to a File**.

⑤ Click **Next**.

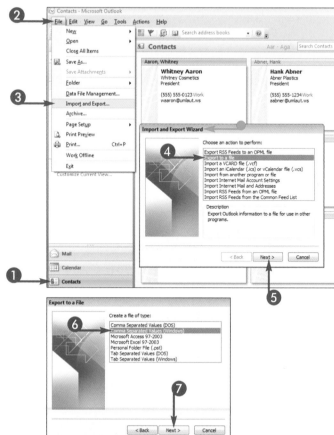

The wizard's Export to a File page opens.

⑥ Click **Comma Separated Values (Windows)**.

⑦ Click **Next**.

8 Click the folder containing the contacts you want to export.

In this example, **Contacts** is selected.

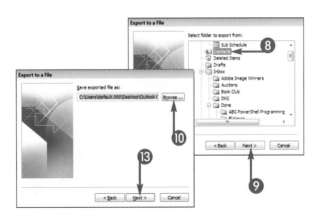

9 Click **Next**.

10 In the next Export to a File page, click **Browse** to indicate where the export file should be saved.

● The Browse dialog box appears.

11 Locate and open the folder in which you want to save the export file.

12 Click **OK** to close the Browse dialog box.

13 Click **Next** in the wizard.

14 Click **Finish**.

Outlook creates the export file, storing it in the folder you specified.

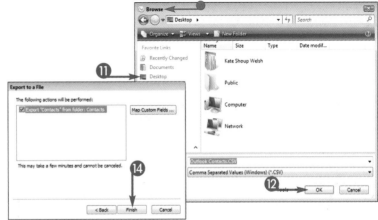

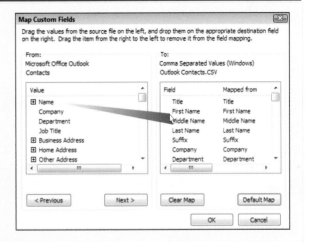

 TIP

What is the Map Custom Fields button for?

Clicking the **Map Custom Fields** button on the last page of the wizard opens a dialog box that enables you to convert, or map, the fields used in your Outlook contacts to equivalent fields used in other contacts-management programs. To do so, click and drag a field listed in the left side of the Map Custom Fields dialog box to its equivalent field on the right. When you finish, click **OK**.

Forward a Contact

You can easily share a contact with someone else by forwarding the Outlook contact entry via e-mail. The recipient of the contact is able to open it in the same way he or she opens any other e-mail attachment.

You can forward an Outlook contact from Contacts, as well as from Outlook's Mail component.

Forward a Contact

① If Contacts is not currently open, click the **Contacts** button in the navigation pane.

Outlook switches to Contacts.

② Double-click the contact you want to share to open it in its own window.

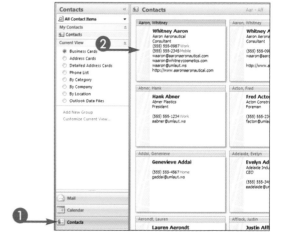

The contact record opens in its own window.

③ Click the **Send** button in the Contact tab's Actions group.

● Click **Send as Business Card** to send the record in business-card form.

● To send the entry as a vCard, click **In Internet Format (vCard)**.

● If you know the recipient uses Outlook as his or her contacts-management program, click **In Outlook Format**.

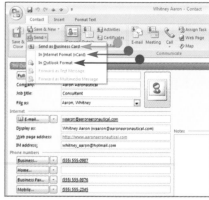

- Outlook launches a Message window, with the contact attached.

④ Type the recipient's e-mail address.

⑤ Type a subject for your message.

⑥ Add any text you want to include in your message.

⑦ Click **Send**.

Note: See Chapter 5 for more about sending e-mail messages.

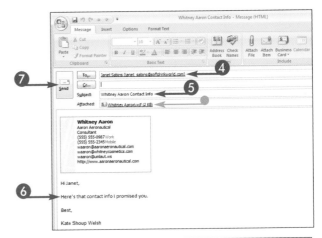

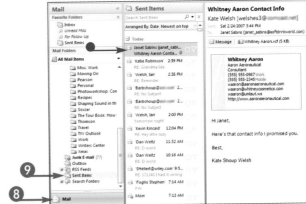

⑧ To verify that the message containing the contact entry was sent, click the **Mail** button.

Outlook switches to Mail.

⑨ In the navigation pane's folder list, click **Sent Items**.

- The message should appear in the list.

 TIPS

What is a vCard?
vCard is a file format designed specifically for exchanging electronic business cards both via e-mail as well as over the World Wide Web. Most e-mail programs support the use of vCards, which have a file extension of .vcf, for exchanging personal information.

Can I forward my contacts any other way?
Depending on your system setup, you may also be able to forward the contact as a text message — for example, to a mobile phone — or as a multimedia message, meaning any files attached to the contact record are included.

Print Your Outlook Contacts

If you know you are traveling to a location where you will not have access to a computer, you can print a hard copy of your Outlook contacts either individually or as part of a list.

Print Your Outlook Contacts

PRINT A LIST OF CONTACTS

1. If you want to print only certain contacts, click them to select them. To print the entire list, skip to Step **2**.

2. Click **File**.

3. Click **Print**.

   The Print dialog box appears.

4. Choose the printer you want to use.

5. Specify the desired print style – **Card**, **Small Booklet**, **Medium Booklet**, **Memo**, or **Phone Directory**.

6. To print all of your contacts, click **All Items**. To print only the entries you selected, click **Only Selected Items**.

7. Type the number of copies you want to print.

8. If you are printing multiple copies, and you want them to be collated, select the **Collate Copies** check box.

9. Click **OK** to print the list.

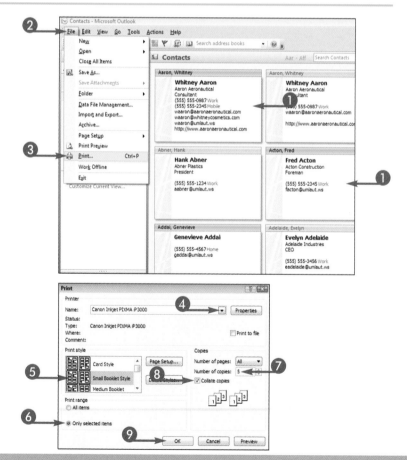

PRINT A SINGLE CONTACT ENTRY

1 Double-click the contact you want to print to open it in its own window.

2 Click the **Print Preview** button (🔍) in the contact window's Quick Access toolbar to open the Print Preview window.

3 Review the layout of the contact information.

4 Click the **Print** button.

5 In the Print dialog box, choose the printer you want to use.

Note: Single contacts can be printed only in Memo style.

6 To print any attachments associated with the contact, select the **Print Attached Files** check box.

7 Type the number of copies you want to print.

8 If you are printing multiple copies, and you want them to be collated, select the **Collate Copies** check box.

9 Click **OK** to print the contact.

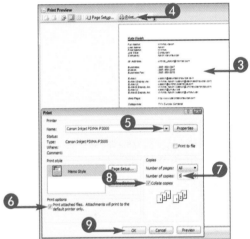

How do I select multiple contacts?

To select multiple contacts that are adjacent to each other in the list, hold down the `Shift` key on your keyboard as you first click the topmost contact you want to select, and then click the bottom-most contact you want to select. To select contacts that are scattered throughout the list, hold down the `Ctrl` key on your keyboard as you click each contact that you want to print.

Where is my Print Preview button?

If the Print Preview button (🔍) is not visible in the contact window's Quick Access toolbar, click the arrow (▾) next to the Quick Access toolbar and choose **Print Preview** (●).

Handling Incoming E-mail

In the last several years, e-mail has become a primary method of communicating — so much so that many people are deluged with messages every day. You can use Outlook's Mail feature to manage your messages and help you avoid being overwhelmed by messages. It enables you to view, print, and organize the messages you receive.

Set Up an E-mail Account

To use Outlook Mail, you must set up an account with and obtain an e-mail address from an Internet service provider (ISP). Then you can use Mail's Add New E-mail Account Wizard to automatically configure Mail to send and receive messages using that address.

Set Up an E-mail Account

CONFIGURE YOUR ACCOUNT AUTOMATICALLY

① If Mail is not currently open, click the **Mail** button in the navigation pane.

Outlook switches to Mail.

② Click **Tools**.

③ Click **Account Settings**.

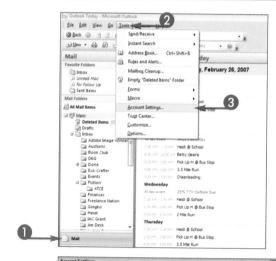

The Account Settings dialog box appears.

④ Click **New**.

The Add New E-mail Account Wizard starts, displaying the Choose E-mail Service page.

⑤ Click the **Microsoft Exchange, POP3, IMAP, or HTTP** option (◎ changes to ◉).

⑥ Click **Next**.

The Add New E-mail Account Wizard's Auto Account Setup page appears.

⑦ Type your name as you want it to appear to others who receive messages from you.

⑧ Type the e-mail address given to you by your ISP.

⑨ Type the password you established with your ISP.

⑩ Type the password a second time to confirm it.

⑪ If you want Outlook to attempt to configure the account automatically, click **Next**.

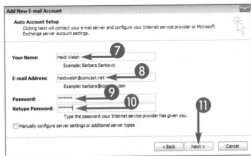

A page appears indicating the progress of the configuration and notifies you when it is complete.

⑫ Click **Finish**.

 TIPS

Can I set up multiple accounts?
You can set up Outlook Mail to handle more than one e-mail account. For example, if you have a personal e-mail account as well as a work account, you can configure Mail to work with both, putting each account in its own folder. Just complete the steps in this task a second time to add a second account, a third time to add a third account, and so on.

How do I remove an account?
To delete an Outlook Mail account, open the **Tools** menu and click **Accounts**. In the Account Settings dialog box, click the account you want to remove, and then click the **Remove** button. When prompted, click **Yes** (◉) to confirm the removal.

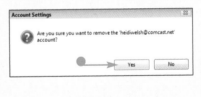

continued

If, for some reason, the Add New E-mail Account Wizard fails to configure your Outlook Mail account automatically, you can set it up manually. To do so, you need your e-mail address, username, password, account type, and the names of your ISP's incoming and outgoing e-mail servers. You can obtain all of this information from your ISP.

Set Up an E-mail Account *(continued)*

CONFIGURE YOUR ACCOUNT MANUALLY

① Repeat Steps **1** to **10** of the preceding task.

The Add New E-mail Account Wizard's Auto Account Setup page appears.

② In the Add New E-mail Account Wizard's Auto Account Setup page, click the **Manually Configure Server Settings or Additional Server Types** check box (☐ changes to ☑).
The text you typed appears grayed out.

③ Click **Next**.

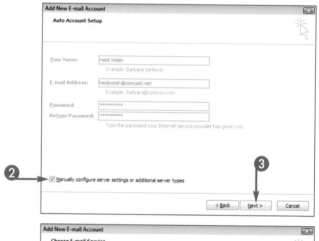

The Add New E-mail Account Wizard's Choose E-mail Service page appears.

④ Click the **Internet E-mail** option (◎ changes to ◉).

⑤ Click **Next**.

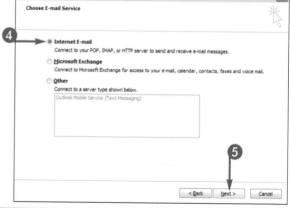

The Add New E-mail Account Wizard's Internet E-mail Settings page appears.

⑥ Click the **Account Type** ▾ and select the type of account you have.

⑦ Type the name of the incoming mail server.

⑧ Type the name of the outgoing mail server.

⑨ Type the username for the e-mail account.

⑩ Type the account's password.

⑪ If you do not want to type your password each time you access this account, click the **Remember Password** check box (☐ changes to ☑).

● To access additional account settings, click the **More Settings** button.

⑫ Click **Next**.

Outlook informs you that you have successfully created the account.

⑬ Click **Finish**.

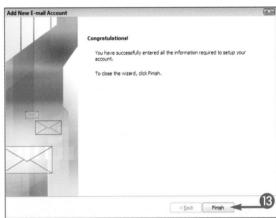

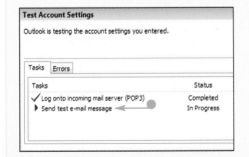

Can I test my account settings?

To test the account settings before completing the configuration process, click the **Test Account Settings** button in the wizard's Internet E-mail Settings screen. Outlook sends a test message to ensure the account is set up correctly (●).

What types of e-mail accounts are there?

This task illustrates how to add a Post Office Protocol version 3 (POP3) e-mail account, although there are other account types, including Internet Message Access Protocol (IMAP) and Hypertext Transfer Protocol (HTTP). Another type of e-mail account is an Exchange account, typically used in a work setting with an IT (information technology) department. To find out which type of account you have, ask your Internet service provider (ISP).

Retrieve and View E-mail Messages

To retrieve e-mail messages sent by others, Outlook must connect to your ISP's mail server. You instruct Outlook to do so by clicking the Send/Receive button in Mail.

If your Outlook window is configured to display the reading pane, you can preview a message in your message list. Alternatively, you can open the message in its own window.

Retrieve and View E-mail Messages

① If Mail is not currently open, click the **Mail** button in the navigation pane.

Outlook switches to Mail.

② Click the **Send/Receive** button.

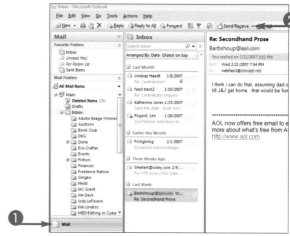

Outlook connects to your ISP's server and downloads any new messages addressed to you.

● Unread messages appear in bold.

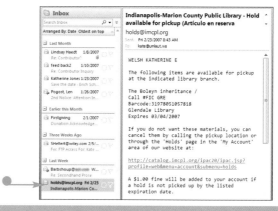

③ Click the message you want to preview or open.

● The contents of the message appear in the reading pane.

Note: *If the reading pane is not currently displayed on-screen, you can reveal it by opening the **View** menu, clicking **Reading Pane**, and selecting either **Right** or **Bottom**, depending on where you want the pane to appear.*

④ If necessary, click and drag the scrollbar down to view the message in its entirety.

⑤ Double-click a message in the message list to open it in its own window.

Note: *Another way to open a message in its own window is to right-click it in the message list and choose **Open** from the menu that appears.*

The message opens in its own window.

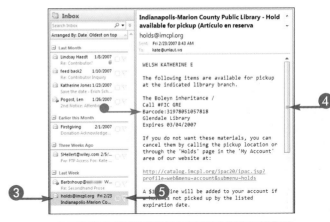

TIPS

Can I automate the Receive operation?
You can set up Outlook to check for new messages automatically at a time interval you specify. (Note that in order for this to work, you need an "always on" Internet connection.) To do so, click **Tools** and then **Options**, click the **Mail Setup** tab, and click **Send/Receive**. Click the **Schedule an Automatic Send/Receive Every *x* Minutes** check box (☐ changes to ☑), type the number of minutes you want to use as an interval for the operation (●), click **Close**, and click **OK**.

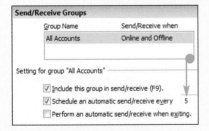

How do I add the sender's information to Contacts?
If you receive a message from a sender whose information has not yet been added to Outlook Contacts, you can add it from directly within the open message. To do so, right-click the sender's e-mail address and choose **Add to Outlook Contacts** (●) from the menu that appears. Outlook launches a New Contact window with as much information as was available filled in; add more info as needed.

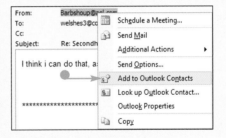

Preview and Open Attachments

If you receive a message with a file attached to it, you can use Outlook to quickly preview the contents of the attached file in the reading pane. Attachments are identified by a special paperclip icon.

Alternatively, if you know you want to work with the attachment immediately, you can open it directly from your message.

Preview and Open Attachments

PREVIEW AN ATTACHMENT

1 Click the message that contains an attachment to display the message's contents in the reading pane.

● The message's contents are displayed.

2 Right-click the attachment, located either immediately below the message's Subject line or as a shortcut icon in the body of the message.

3 Click **Preview**.

● In the reading pane, Outlook alerts you that only those attachments from a trustworthy source should be previewed.

4 Click **Preview File**.

● The contents of the attachment appear in the reading pane.

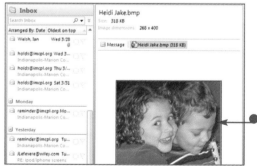

OPEN AN ATTACHMENT

1 Click the message that contains an attachment to display the message's contents in the reading pane.

The message's contents are displayed.

2 Right-click the attachment, located either immediately below the message's Subject line or as a shortcut icon in the body of the message.

3 Click **Open**.

● The Opening Mail Attachment dialog box appears.

4 Click **Open**.

The file opens in the appropriate program (assuming that program is installed on your PC).

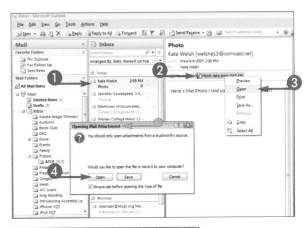

 TIPS

How do I save an attachment?

To save, rather than open, an attachment, display the message that contains the attachment in the reading pane, right-click the attachment, and choose **Save As**. The Save Attachment dialog box appears; locate and select the folder in which you want to save the file and click **Save**.

How do I add attached electronic business cards to contacts?

If the attachment you received is an electronic business card file, it appears both as a file attachment under the Subject line and as a graphic of a business card that displays the file's contents in the body of the message. To save the information in the electronic business card as a contact, right-click the business-card graphic and choose **Add to Outlook Contacts** (●). The information in the business card appears in its own contact window; click **Save & Close** to save it.

Print an E-mail Message

Although Outlook is designed to store your e-mail messages in electronic form, sometimes there is no substitute for a printout. Fortunately, Outlook makes it easy to print hard copies of messages.

Note that in order to print an e-mail message, your computer must be attached to a printer, and that printer's software must be installed.

Print an E-mail Message

① In the message list, double-click the message you want to print.

The message appears in its own window.

② Click the **Print Preview** button (🖺) in the message window's Quick Launch toolbar.

● If the Print Preview button (🖺) button is not visible, click ▾ on the right edge of the Quick Launch toolbar and choose **Print Preview**.

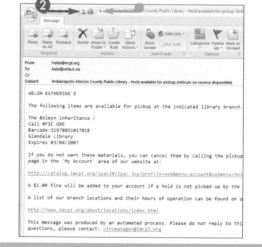

A Print Preview window opens, displaying how the message will look on paper.

③ Review the layout of the message.

④ Click the **Print** button.

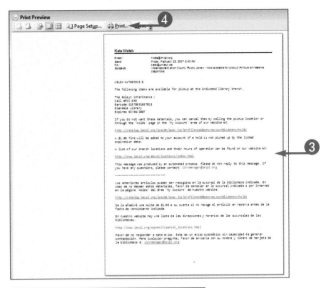

The Print dialog box appears.

⑤ Choose the printer you want to use.

⑥ To print any attachments associated with the contact, click the **Print Attached Files** check box (☐ changes to ☑).

⑦ Type the number of copies you want to print.

⑧ If you are printing multiple copies, and you want them to be collated, click the **Collate Copies** check box (☐ changes to ☑).

⑨ Click **OK** to print the message.

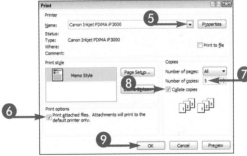

TIPS

Can I change the page setup?

A quick way to make minor changes to the way your message looks is to click the **Page Setup** button, either in the Print Preview window or in the Print dialog box. Doing so opens the Page Setup dialog box, which includes options for changing the font, paper size, and more.

Is there a faster way to print?

If you know you do not need to preview your message first, and you do not need to change any print settings, you can print by clicking the **Print** button (🖨) in the message window's Quick Access toolbar. (If that button is not visible, click 🔽 in the top-left area of the window and choose **QuickPrint**.) Alternatively, click the message in the message list and click the **Print** toolbar button (🖨).

Mark a Message as Read or Unread

When a message has not been opened in its own window, it appears bold in the message list, indicating that it is *unread*. Opening the message removes the bold formatting. You can mark a message you have read as unread to make it bold again; you might do this for messages that still require your attention.

Mark a Message as Read or Unread

MARK A MESSAGE AS UNREAD

1 Right-click the message in the list that you want to mark as unread.

2 Click **Mark as Unread**.

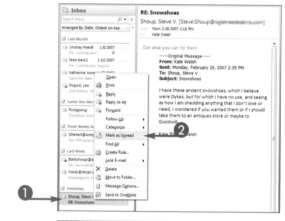

- The message appears bold in the message list.

- When a folder, such as the Inbox, contains any unread messages, the number of unread messages appears in parentheses next to the folder's name in the folder list.

Note: *You can also mark a message that is open in its own window as unread by clicking* **Mark as Unread** *in the message window's Ribbon.*

Note: *If you want to view all unread messages in one place, Outlook stores a copy of all unread messages in the Unread Mail folder, located under the Search Folders folder.*

MARK A MESSAGE AS READ

1️⃣ Right-click the message in the list that you want to mark as read.

2️⃣ Click **Mark as Read**.

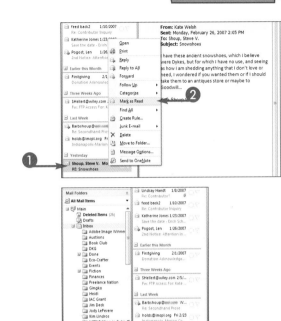

● The bold formatting is removed from the message in the message list.

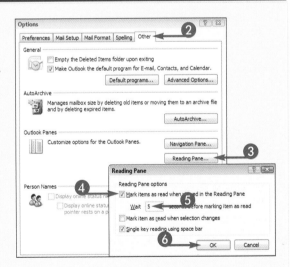

Can a message be marked as read when displayed in the reading pane?

Yes. You can configure Outlook to automatically mark a message as read after it is displayed in the reading pane by doing the following:

1️⃣ Open the **Tools** menu and click **Options**.

2️⃣ In the Options dialog box, click the **Other** tab.

3️⃣ Click the **Reading Pane** button.

4️⃣ In the Reading Pane dialog box, click the **Mark Items As Read When Viewed in the Reading Pane** check box (☐ changes to ☑).

5️⃣ Type the number of seconds you want the message to have been displayed in the reading pane before it is marked as read.

6️⃣ Click **OK** to close both dialog boxes.

Flag a Message for Follow-Up

Flagging a message helps you remember to follow up on it. Suppose your boss sends you a message asking to gather data for an important meeting. Flagging the message creates a visual reminder within Mail, and adds the message to your task list.

In addition to flagging messages you receive from others, you can also flag messages you send.

Flag a Message for Follow-Up

FLAG A MESSAGE FOR FOLLOW-UP

1. Right-click the grayed-out flag in the message you want to flag in the message list.

2. Specify when you need to follow up on the message.

● Click **Custom** if none of the entries in the menu suits your needs. Doing so opens a dialog box that enables you to set your own follow-up parameters.

● A colored flag appears in the message's entry in the message list.

● The message is added to your task list.

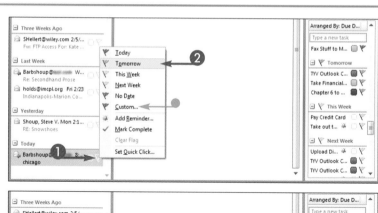

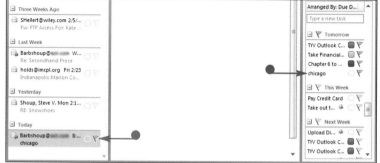

CLEAR A FLAG

① Right-click the flag you want to clear.

② Click **Clear Flag**.

● Another option is to click **Mark Complete**. When you do, the flag marking the e-mail message in the message list converts to a check mark, and the message is removed from the task list.

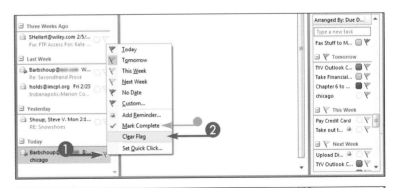

● The flag is grayed out.

● The message is removed to your task list.

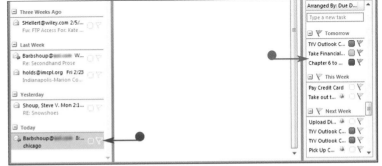

TIPS

Can I expedite the flagging process?

One way to speed up the flagging process is to simply click the grayed-out flag that appears in the message entry in the message list. By default, the flag added requires follow-up today. To change the default follow-up period, right-click a message in the message list, click **Follow Up**, and then **Set Quick Click**. In the Set Quick Click dialog box that appears, open the drop-down list and click the desired follow-up period (●).

Can I view all flagged messages at once?

Outlook stores a copy of all your flagged messages in a special folder called For Follow Up (●), under the Search Folders folder. Another way to view all flagged messages as a group is to sort your message list by clicking **Arranged By** at the top of the list and clicking either **Flag: Start Date** or **Flag: Due Date**.

continued

To remind yourself to follow up on an e-mail, you can set a *reminder*. That way, Outlook displays a special dialog box before the follow-up task is due to remind you.

Flag a Message for Follow-Up *(continued)*

SET A REMINDER FOR A FLAGGED MESSAGE

① Right-click the flag on the message for which you want to set a reminder.

② Click **Add Reminder**.

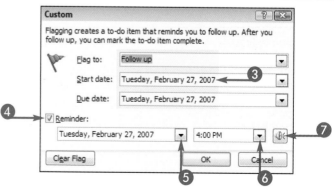

The Custom dialog box appears.

③ Verify that the information about the flag is correct.

④ Verify that the Reminder check box is selected.

⑤ Specify the day on which you want to receive the reminder.

⑥ Specify the time at which you want to receive the reminder.

⑦ If you want Outlook to play a sound when it displays the reminder, click the **Sound** button (◁ℰ).

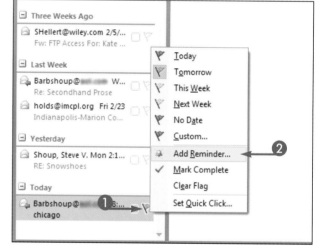

- The Reminder Sound dialog box appears.

⑧ Verify that the Play This Sound check box is checked.

- If you want Outlook to play a different sound from the one listed, click the **Browse** button, and in the dialog box that appears, locate and select the sound you want to use.

⑨ Click **OK** to close the Reminder Sound dialog box.

⑩ Click **OK** to close the Custom dialog box.

- On the date and time you specified, Outlook displays the reminder.

⑪ If you want Outlook to send you a second reminder, click **Snooze**.

⑫ By default, Outlook sends a second reminder in five minutes; to change this number, open the drop-down list next to the **Snooze** button and select the desired interval.

⑬ Click **Dismiss** to close the reminder.

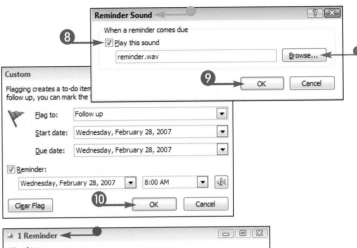

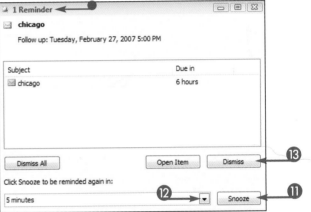

TIPS

Can I view the follow-up information for a message?

To see a message's follow-up information, double-click the message in the message list to open it; follow-up details, as well as whether you have replied to the message, appear just below the Ribbon.

Will others see the flag and reminder information?

By default, if you reply to a message for which you have set a flag and/or a reminder, the recipient of your reply also sees the flag and/or reminder information. To remove it, open the message to which you want to reply. In the message's window, click **Reply** or **Reply All**. In the Ribbon's Message tab, in the Options group, click **Follow Up**. Click **Flag for Recipients**. A Custom dialog box appears; click the **Flag for Recipients** check box (☑ changes to ▢). Click **OK** to close the Custom dialog box, and compose and send your reply as normal. (You learn how to compose and reply to messages in Chapter 5.)

By default, messages are displayed in the message list by date, with more recent messages appearing at the bottom. If this arrangement does not suit you, you can sort your messages by another criterion, such as by sender, by category, and more. In addition, you can create custom search parameters.

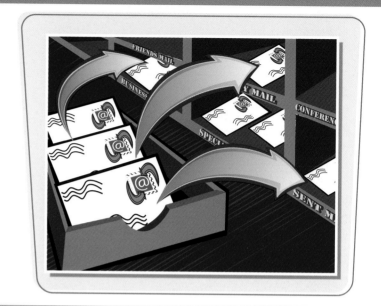

Sort Messages

PERFORM A SIMPLE SORT

1. At the top of the message list, click **Arranged By**.

2. Choose the criterion by which you want to sort the messages.

   Outlook sorts the messages by the criterion you select.

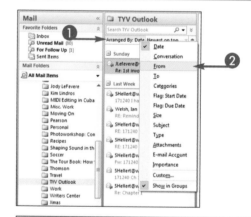

PERFORM A CUSTOM SORT

1. At the top of the message list, click **Arranged By**.

2. Click **Custom**.

● The Customize View dialog box appears.

3. Click **Sort**.

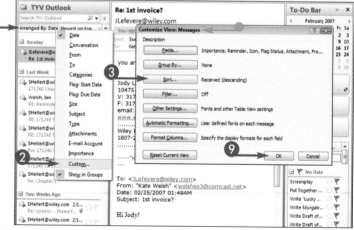

● The Sort dialog box appears.

④ Click the **Sort Items By** 🔽.

⑤ Choose the parameter by which you want to sort (here, **From**).

⑥ If you want messages to appear in A-to–Z order, click the **Ascending** option; to display them from Z to A, click the **Descending** option.

⑦ Repeat Steps **5** and **6** in as many **Then By** fields as necessary to enter the rest of your sort parameters.

⑧ Click **OK** to close the Sort dialog box.

⑨ Click **OK** to close the Customize View dialog box.

● Your messages are sorted accordingly.

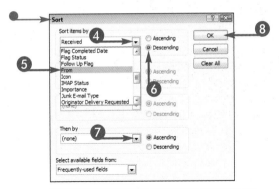

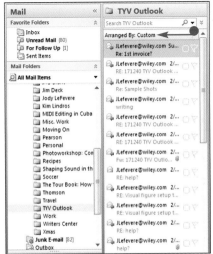

How can I undo a custom sort?

To undo a custom sort, simply click **Custom** at the top of the message list and choose the new criterion by which you want to sort.

How does grouping work?

By default, Outlook arranges your messages in groups. For example, if the criterion by which you have sorted is Date, then all messages received on a particular date, week, or month are grouped (depending on how recently the message was received). You can collapse (●) a group (that is, hide all the messages within the group, showing only the group header) or expand (●) a group (revealing the messages that were hidden when the group was collapsed) by clicking the plus (⊞) or minus (⊟) button, respectively.

Organize Messages Using Rules

Suppose you want all messages you receive from a specific sender to be filed in a particular folder automatically. To accomplish that, as well as many other automated Mail tasks, you can set up a *rule*. Any messages that meet the criteria defined in the rule are handled in the manner you specify.

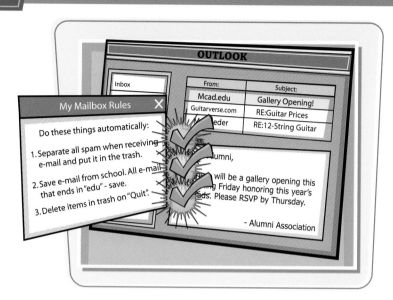

1. With Outlook Mail open, click **Tools**.

2. Click **Rules and Alerts**.

● The Rules and Alerts dialog box appears.

3. Click **New Rule**.

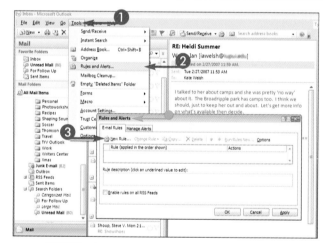

The Rules Wizard opens.

4. To move messages from a certain sender to a folder, click **Move Messages from Someone to a Folder**.

5. Click **Next**.

⑥ Click a check box next to the condition that meets your needs (☐ changes to ☑).

In this example, **From People or Distribution List** is selected.

⑦ To specify the sender to whom the rule applies, click the **People or Distribution List** link.

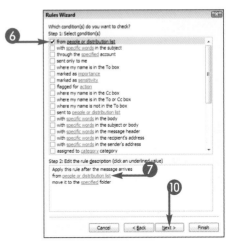

The Rule Address dialog box appears.

⑧ Double-click the names of any people or distribution lists you want to adhere to the rule.

● The names you double-click appear in the From field.

⑨ Click **OK** in the Rule Address dialog box.

⑩ Click **Next** in the Rules Wizard.

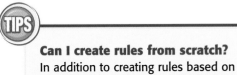

Can I create rules from scratch?
In addition to creating rules based on predefined templates provided by Outlook, you can also create them from scratch. To do so, launch the Rules Wizard, select the desired option under Start from a Blank Rule, click **Next**, and follow the on-screen prompts.

Can I import rules from previous versions of Outlook?
If you established rules in an earlier version of Outlook, you can import those rules into this version. (Note that in order to import your rules from a previous version of Outlook, you must first *export* them from that earlier version.) To access the tools for importing and exporting rules, as well as for upgrading any rules you import for better performance in Outlook 2007, click the **Options** button in the Rules and Alerts dialog box to open the Options dialog box.

continued

You are not limited to creating rules that place messages from a certain sender in a specific folder. For example, you might create a rule that dictates that all messages from a particular sender (for example, your boss) be flagged for immediate attention.

You can also set *exceptions* – that is, situations in which the rule you create is ignored.

Organize Messages Using Rules *(continued)*

⑪ To choose the folder to which messages from the specified sender should be moved, click the **Specified** link in the Rules Wizard.

● The Rules and Alerts dialog box appears.

⑫ Navigate to and select the folder in which you want to save messages from the selected senders.

⑬ Click **OK** in the Rules and Alerts dialog box.

⑭ Click **Next** in the Rules Wizard.

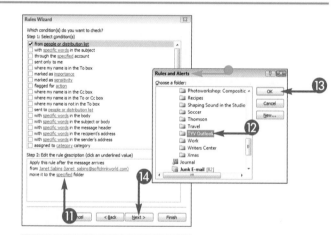

⑮ Click the check box next to any additional actions you want the rule to apply (☐ changes to ☑).

⑯ Click **Next**.

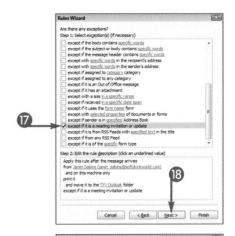

⑰ If there are circumstances in which you want your new rule to be ignored, click any applicable check boxes (☐ changes to ☑).

⑱ Click **Next**.

⑲ To change the default name for the rule, type over it in the Specify a Name for This Rule field.

● To apply the rule to messages already in your inbox, click the **Run This Rule Now on Messages Already in Inbox** check box (☐ changes to ☑).

⑳ Verify that the Turn On this Rule check box is checked.

㉑ Review the rule description.

㉒ Click **Finish**.

㉓ Click **OK** to close the Rules and Alerts dialog box.

Outlook creates the rule and applies it to messages meeting the criteria you specified.

Is there a quicker way to create a rule?
If you want to create a rule that applies to a certain sender, and it so happens you have a message from that sender in your message list, you can do the following to expedite the creation of the rule:

① Right-click a message from the sender to which you want to apply the rule and click Create Rule in the shortcut menu that appears.

② The Create Rule dialog box appears. Under **When I Get E-mail with All the Selected Conditions**, click the check box next to the necessary conditions. The **From** check box is selected here.

③ Under Do the Following, click the check box next to the actions you want Outlook to take when the conditions are met.

④ Depending on what options you select, Outlook may prompt you for additional information; respond as necessary.

⑤ Click **OK**. Outlook creates the rule.

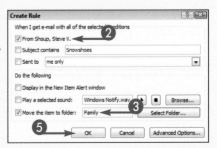

Filter Junk E-mail

You can use Outlook Mail's Junk E-mail Filter to automatically divert junk mail, also called *spam*, from your inbox into a special Junk E-Mail folder using settings you specify. Not having to sift through dozens of spam e-mails each day to locate "real" messages is a real timesaver!

Filter Junk E-mail

CHANGE JUNK E-MAIL FILTER SETTINGS

By default, Outlook Mail applies a low level of protection from junk e-mail, but you can change these settings.

① To change the level of protection, click **Actions**.

② Click **Junk E-mail**.

③ Click **Junk E-mail Options**.

The Junk E-mail Options dialog box appears.

● Click an option to specify the level of protection from junk e-mail you want.

● Select this check box if you want Outlook to delete junk e-mail messages instead of moving them to the Junk E-mail folder.

● Select this check box if you want Outlook to disable links in suspicious messages.

● Select this check box if you want Outlook to warn you if it detects a suspicious e-mail address.

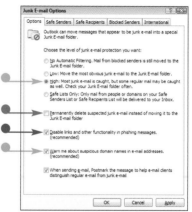

● Click here to apply a postmark to outgoing messages.

Note: *You can learn more about postmarks in Chapter 5.*

④ Click **OK**.

Outlook applies the settings you select to the Junk E-mail Filter.

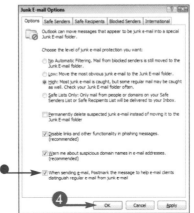

BLOCK MESSAGES FROM A SENDER

If Outlook allows a spam message through, you can block subsequent messages from the sender.

① Right-click the message.

② Click **Junk E-mail**.

③ Click **Add Sender to Blocked Senders List**.

● Outlook notifies you that the sender has been added to your Blocked Senders list, and that the message has been moved to the Junk E-mail folder.

④ Click **OK**.

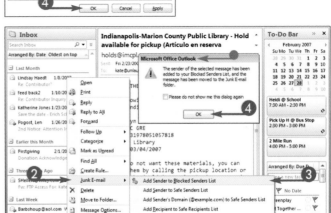

Are there other ways to block senders?
If you know the e-mail address of a sender whose messages you want to block, but have not yet received a message from that person, you can add the e-mail address to the Blocked Senders list from within the Junk E-mail Options dialog box.

① Open the **Actions** menu, click **Junk E-mail**, and then click **Junk E-mail Options**.

② In the Junk E-mail Options dialog box, click the **Blocked Senders** tab.

③ Click **Add**.

④ Type the e-mail address you want to block.

⑤ Click **OK** to close the dialog boxes.

continued

Periodically check the Junk E-mail folder to ensure that no authentic messages have been diverted. If one is, mark it as "not junk" to move the message to the message list and, optionally, add the sender to your Safe Senders list. You can also ensure that any sender listed in Contacts is considered safe by the Junk E-mail Filter.

Filter Junk E-mail *(continued)*

MARK A MESSAGE AS NOT JUNK

① Click the **Junk E-mail** folder in the folder list.

Outlook displays the contents of the Junk E-mail folder in the message list.

② Right-click the message you want to mark as not junk.

③ Click **Junk E-mail**.

④ Click **Mark as Not Junk**.

The Mark as Not Junk dialog box appears.

⑤ To always trust e-mail from the sender, verify that this check box is checked.

⑥ Click **OK**.

Outlook moves the message to your inbox.

MARK ALL CONTACTS AS SAFE SENDERS

1 To change the level of protection, click **Actions**.

2 Click **Junk E-mail**.

3 Click **Junk E-mail Options**.

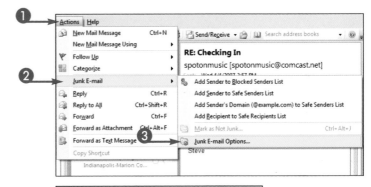

The Junk E-mail Options dialog box opens.

4 Click the **Safe Senders** tab.

5 Verify that the **Also Trust E-mail from My Contacts** check box is checked.

● Optionally, click the **Automatically Add People I E-mail to the Safe Senders List** check box (changes to).

6 Click **OK**.

Does Outlook protect me from phishing?

Phishing typically involves an e-mail message that appears to be from a legitimate source such as a bank, informing the user that his or her account information must be updated. When the provided link is clicked, however, the user is directed to a bogus site designed to mimic a trusted site in order to steal personal information. Outlook's anti-phishing features help detect these fraudulent messages automatically, disabling any links in messages it deems suspicious and alerting you to the problem in the message window's InfoBar.

Clean Up
Your Mailbox

If you find that your mailbox is so full that it is impossible to navigate, you can clean it using Outlook's Mailbox Cleanup feature.

It enables you to find items to delete or move, archive old items, and empty the Deleted Items folder.

Clean Up Your Mailbox

① Click **Tools**.

② Click **Mailbox Cleanup**.

● The Mailbox Cleanup dialog box appears.

③ To see how much space your mailbox is currently consuming on your hard drive, click **View Mailbox Size**.

● The Folder Size dialog box appears, indicating the amount of space occupied by your mailbox.

④ Click **Close**.

⑤ To see how much space is currently occupied by items in the Deleted Items folder, click **View Deleted Items Size**.

● The Folder Size dialog box appears, this time indicating the amount of space occupied by the Deleted Items folder.

⑥ Click **Close** to close the Folder Size dialog box.

⑦ To empty the Deleted Items folder, permanently removing the items it contains from your computer, click **Empty**.

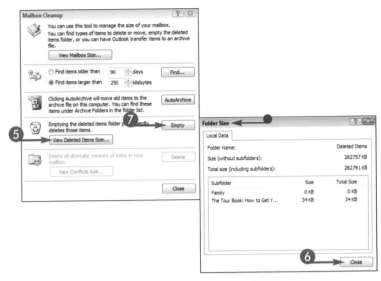

⑧ When prompted to confirm the operation, click **Yes**.

Outlook removes the items in the Deleted Items folder.

Is there a quicker way to empty the Deleted Items folder?

Another way to empty the Deleted Items folder is to click **Tools** and then **Empty Deleted Items Folder**. When Outlook prompts you to confirm the operation, click **Yes**.

Can I archive Outlook items?

You can archive older Outlook messages. To do so, click **AutoArchive** in the Mailbox Cleanup dialog box. When you do, Outlook moves all old Outlook items to a special folder, accessible under Archive Folders in the folder list.

Composing and Sending E-mail Messages

To: Jon Warner
From: Ann Burroughs
Subject: Lovely day & Workflow
Message:
Jon,
It's a beautiful day, sunny and
bright and optimistic, so I hate
to bother you with this, but I'm
in need of more work. The
editors were supposed to cycle
some down here this morning,
but I imagine they were overcome
by Spring Fever, too. Could you
look into this?
Thanks, and have a sunny day,
Ann

Of course, in addition to receiving e-mail messages via Outlook Mail, you can also send e-mail messages. One way to send a message is to reply to one you have received; another is to forward a message you have received to a third party. In addition, you can compose and send brand-new messages.

Reply to a Message

If you receive a message, you can quickly and easily reply to it from within the message window. If the message to which you are replying was sent to multiple people, you can click Reply All in the message window to send your reply to everyone on the list; alternatively, click Reply to send your response to the sender only.

Reply to a Message

① In the Mail message list, double-click the message to which you want to respond to open it in its own window.

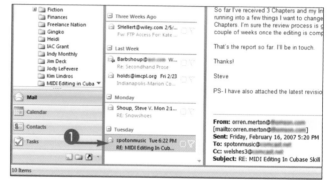

The message opens in its own window.

② To reply to the sender and to any other recipients of the original message, click **Reply All**, as shown here.

To reply to the sender only, click **Reply**.

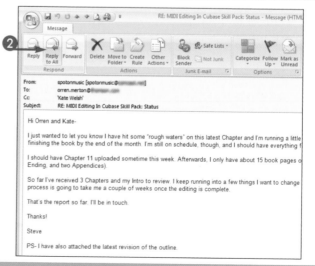

A new message window opens with the original message text displayed.

● The e-mail addresses of the sender and other recipients of the original message appear in the To field.

● "RE:" is added to the subject of the message, indicating that this message is a reply.

③ Type your reply.

④ Click **Send**.

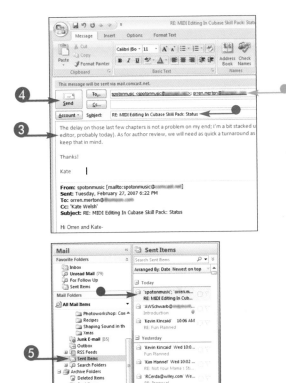

Outlook sends the reply.

Note: *You might need to close the original message window. To do so, click the **Close** button (✕) in the top-right corner.*

⑤ To verify that the message has been sent, click the **Sent Items** folder in the folder list to open it.

● The message is displayed in the message list.

TIPS

What if I forget whether I have replied to a message?

If you cannot remember whether you have responded to a message, view the message's InfoBar — that is, the blue bar at the top of the message — to see what actions have been taken. If you have indeed responded, you can view the reply — and any other messages that are related to the original one — by clicking the InfoBar and choosing **Find Related Messages**.

Can I add a reminder to a message I send?

Whether you are replying to, forwarding, or creating a brand-new message, you can flag it to remind the recipient to take action. To do so, click the **Message** tab on the message window's Ribbon. In the Options group, click **Follow Up** and choose **Add Reminder**. The Custom dialog box appears; click the **Flag for Recipients** check box (☐ changes to ☑), choose the type of flag you want to apply, click the **Reminder** check box (☐ changes to ☑), choose the day and time on which the reminder should be displayed, and click **OK**.

Forward a Message

Suppose you receive an e-mail message that you want to share with someone else. For example, maybe you received a message from your boss that needs to be shared with your employees. To do so, you can simply *forward* the message, adding your own text to the message if desired.

Forward a Message

1 In the Mail message list, double-click the message you want to forward to open it in its own window.

The message opens in its own window.

2 Click **Forward**.

A new message window opens.

- "FW:" is added to the subject of the message, indicating that this message has been forwarded.

③ Type the recipient's e-mail address.

Note: *You learn the various ways to add recipients to a message in the next task.*

④ Type any text you want to add to the forwarded message.

⑤ Click **Send**.

Outlook sends the message.

Note: *You might need to close the original message window. To do so, click the **Close** button (⨯) in the top-right corner.*

⑥ To verify that the message has been sent, click the **Sent Items** folder in the folder list to open it.

- The message is displayed in the message list.

 TIPS

Can I forward a message as an attachment?

Rather than forwarding a message as body text, you can forward it as an attachment. To do so, select the message you want to forward in the message list, click **Actions**, and choose **Forward as Attachment**.

Can I prevent my messages from being forwarded to others?

If your message includes sensitive information, you might want to limit others from forwarding it. To do so, click the down arrow to the right of the **Permissions** button (🔳) in the Message tab's Options group and choose **Do Not Forward**.

Compose and Send a New Message

In addition to replying to or forwarding messages you receive, you can also start your own thread of messages by creating a new message.

When composing an e-mail message, especially for work, it is usually best to keep it short. Your subject line and the body of your message should be clear and concise. Also, avoid spelling and grammatical errors.

Compose and Send a New Message

① In Outlook Mail, click the **New** toolbar button.

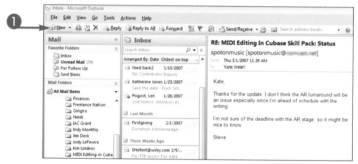

A new message window opens.

② To obtain your recipient's e-mail address from Outlook Contacts, click the **To** button.

Note: *If you know the recipient's e-mail address, you can skip this step and simply type it in the To field.*

● The Select Names dialog box appears, listing your contacts.

③ Click the entry for the desired recipient.

④ Click **To**.

● The recipient's information is added to the To field.

Note: *Repeat Steps 3 and 4 as many times as necessary to add all the intended recipients.*

⑤ Click **OK**.

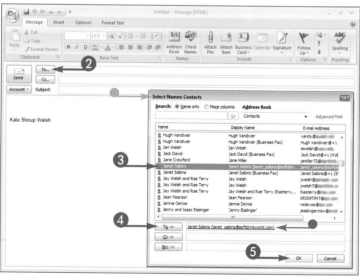

● The recipient's e-mail address appears in the message window's To field.

⑥ Type a subject for your message.

⑦ Type your message.

Note: *Be aware that your recipient might misinterpret your sarcastic repartee as offensive chatter. To convey that you are just kidding around, consider using an emoticon (the ubiquitous smiley-face).*

⑧ Click **Send**.

Note: *Sometimes, being able to write and send an e-mail message in an instant is a bad thing. If you are angry at the recipient, give yourself time to cool down before sending a message.*

Outlook Mail sends the message.

⑨ To verify that the message has been sent, click the **Sent Items** folder in the folder list to open it.

● The message is displayed in the message list.

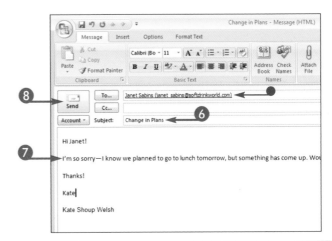

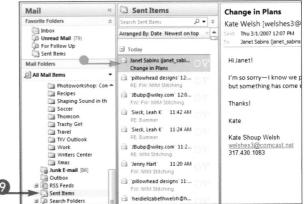

TIPS

Can I send a message from a different account?

Suppose you have multiple e-mail accounts — say, one for work and one for home. Or maybe another person shares your computer and both of you have set up e-mail accounts in Outlook. If you want to reply to, forward, or send a message from the alternate account instead of the default one, you can; simply click the **Account** button (●) below the Send button in the message window and choose the desired account.

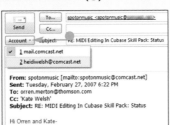

Can I send carbon copies and blind carbon copies of my message?

To add another recipient on your message, add his or her e-mail address to the message's CC or BCC field. To do so, click the copy recipient's name in the Select Names dialog box and click either the **CC** or **BCC** button. (You use the BCC feature to copy another person on your message without having his or her name appear among in the list of recipients in order to protect his or her privacy.)

Save a Message as a Draft

Suppose you are composing an e-mail but you run out of time to finish. Rather than sending it off before it is ready, or losing what you have written so far, you can save the message as a *draft*. That way, when you are ready to resume writing, you can reopen the message and start where you left off.

Save a Message as a Draft

① Compose as much of your message as you have time to complete.

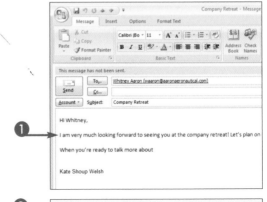

② Click the **Office** button in the message window.

③ Click **Save**.

④ Click the **Close** button (⊠) in the upper-right corner of the message window to close it.

Outlook saves the message in the Drafts folder.

⑤ When you are ready to resume writing, click the **Drafts** folder in the folder list.

● The saved message appears in the message list.

⑥ Double-click the saved message to open it in its own window.

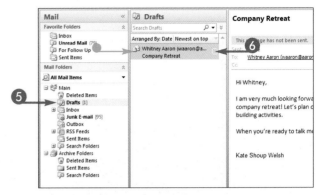

⑦ Finish composing the message and send it.

After you send the message, it is removed from the Drafts folder.

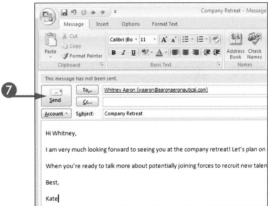

TIPS

What if I finish my message but want to wait to send it?

If you finish typing a message but are not yet ready to send it, you can either save it as a draft using the steps here or delay the delivery to a time you specify. To delay delivery of a message, click the message window's **Options** tab and, in the More Options group, click **Delay Delivery**. The Message Options dialog box appears; ensure that the **Do Not Deliver Before** check box is checked (●), use the corresponding fields to select the date and time of delivery, and click **Close**.

Does Outlook auto-save messages?

Outlook performs AutoSave on e-mail messages during the composition process. By default, a copy of the message is saved to the Drafts folder every three minutes. To change this time interval, click **Tools**, **Options**, **E-mail Options**, and then **Advanced E-mail Options**. In the **AutoSave Unset Every x Minutes** field, type a number from 1 to 99 (●).

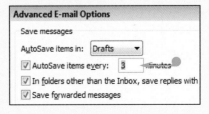

Create a Distribution List

If you frequently send e-mails to the same group of contacts — for example, to your team members at work — you can place those people in a *distribution list*. Any time you need to send a message to the group, you can simply type the name of the distribution list in the message's To field instead of adding each contact individually.

Create a Distribution List

① In the Outlook Mail window, click **File**.

② Click **New**.

③ Click **Distribution List**.

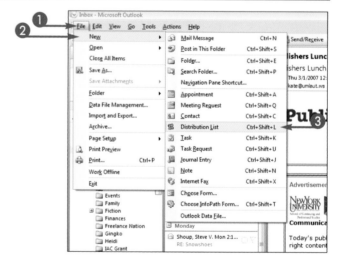

● An empty distribution list window opens.

④ Click **Select Members**.

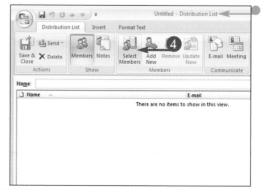

The Select Members: Contacts dialog box appears.

⑤ While holding down the `Ctrl` key on your keyboard, click each contact you want to include in your distribution list. (This is called *Ctrl-clicking*.)

⑥ Click **Members**.

● The contacts you Ctrl-clicked appear in the Members field.

⑦ Click **OK**.

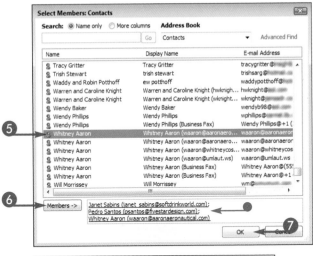

● The contacts you selected appear in the distribution list window.

⑧ Type a name for the distribution list.

⑨ Click **Save & Close**.

Outlook creates the distribution list.

TIPS

How do I send a message to the distribution list?

To send a message to the distribution list, click the To button in the message window and, in the Select Names dialog box that appears, click the list's name (●).

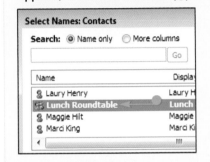

What if I want to include someone who is not in Contacts?

These steps assume that each person you want to include in your distribution list is already listed in Contacts. If not, click **Add New** in the distribution list window and, in the dialog box that appears, type the necessary information and click **OK**. If you want to add the person to Contacts as well as to the distribution list, click the **Add to Contacts** check box (☐ changes to ☑).

Attach a File

If you need to send a file to someone — for example, a document containing important information for work — you can add the document to your e-mail message as an attachment. When your message is received, the recipient can then open the attached file on his or her computer (provided the necessary software is installed to read the file).

Attach a File

1 Compose your message.

2 Click **Attach File**.

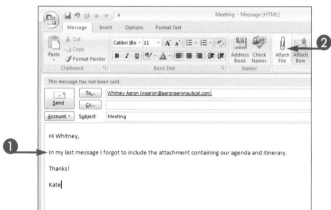

The Insert File dialog box appears.

3 Navigate to the folder containing the file you want to attach and click the file to select it.

4 Click **Insert**.

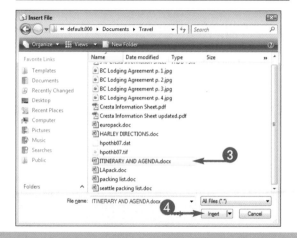

● Outlook attaches the file to your message.

⑤ Click **Send**.

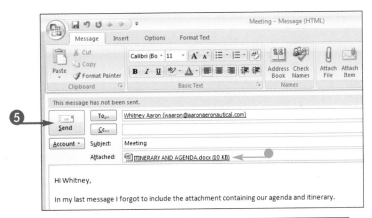

⑥ To verify that the message and attachment were sent, click the **Sent Items** folder in the folder list.

● The attachment is indicated by a paper-clip icon.

Note: Not all types of files can be attached to an Outlook message. File types deemed dangerous, due to their ability to spread viruses and otherwise wreak havoc, are not allowed. For specifics as to what types of files are prohibited, see Outlook's Help information.

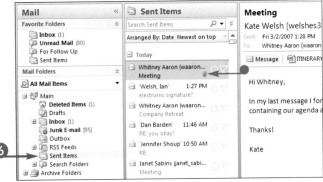

TIPS

Can I attach Outlook items to a message?

In addition to attaching files such as documents or photos to an e-mail message, you can also attach Outlook items such as e-mail messages, tasks, calendar entries, and so on. To do so, click the **Attach Item** button, located next to the Attach File button. The Insert Item dialog box appears; click the folder containing the item you want to attach (●), click the item to select it (●), and click **OK**.

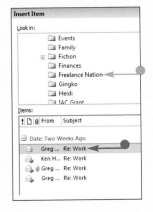

What if my message is urgent?

If your message is particularly urgent, you can indicate this by setting its priority level to High. To do so, click the **High-Priority** button (⚠), found in the message window's Message tab in the Options group.

Insert a Photo

If you want to share an image file, such as one containing a digital photograph, with someone without forcing that person to go through the hassle of opening it as an attachment, you can simply insert the image file (as well as other types of files) into the body of your message.

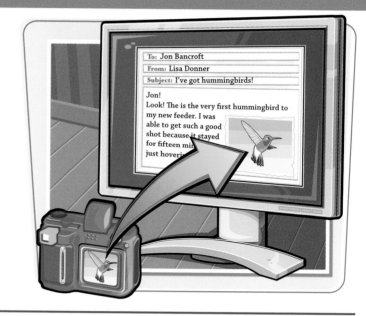

Insert a Photo

1. Compose your message.

2. Place your cursor in the spot where you want the image to appear.

3. Click the **Insert** tab.

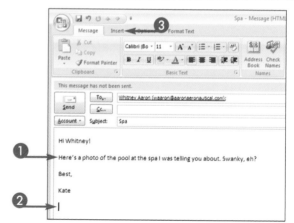

4. Click **Picture**.

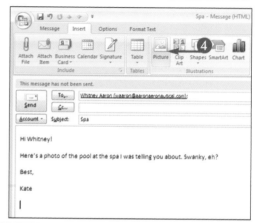

The Insert Picture dialog box appears.

⑤ Locate and click the image file you want to include.

⑥ Click **Insert**.

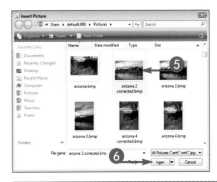

● The picture is inserted into the e-mail message.

● Notice that a special Format tab is displayed in the message window's Ribbon; settings on this tab relate to editing images.

⑦ Click **Send**.

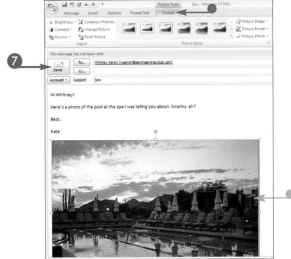

 TIPS

Why can my recipient not see the picture I inserted?

If your recipient's e-mail program cannot process HTML or Rich Text messages, then your recipient will not be able to see the picture you inserted in your message.

Am I limited to inserting my own pictures?

You can also insert *clip art* — that is, digital graphics, designs, and other types of images — in your messages. Outlook includes several clip-art files for your use; in addition, Outlook can download clip art from Office Online. To insert clip art into a message, click the spot in the message where you want the image to appear, click the **Clip Art** button in the message window's Insert tab, and, in the Clip Art pane, search for images by typing a keyword (●) and clicking **Go**. Click any of the images displayed to insert it in your message.

Proofread Your Message

After composing your message, take a moment to proofread it using Outlook's reference resources — especially if the message is bound for your boss or another work colleague.

Outlook's resources go beyond a simple spell-check; also available is a research reference, a thesaurus, and more.

Proofread Your Message

① Compose your message, being sure to include your recipient's e-mail address in the To field and descriptive text in the Subject field.

● Notice that Outlook displays red squiggly lines under certain words; these indicate that the word is misspelled.

② On the message window's Message tab, in the Proofing group, click the **Spelling** button.

The Spelling and Grammar dialog box appears, highlighting the first spelling error and suggesting replacement text.

● Click **Ignore Once** to ignore the error.

● Click **Ignore All** to ignore all instances of the error.

● If the highlighted word appears as you intended, but simply is not recognized by Outlook, click **Add to Dictionary**.

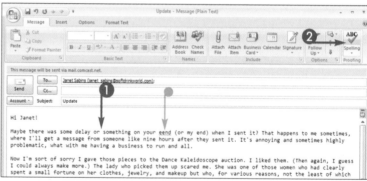

● To change this instance of the error, click **Change**.

● To change all instances of the error, click **Change All**.

● Click **AutoCorrect** if you want Outlook to handle corrections automatically (that is, without your input).

● If you want Outlook to also check for grammatical errors, click the **Check Grammar** check box (☐ changes to ☑).

After you respond to each of Outlook's suggestions, it informs you the spelling and grammar check is complete.

③ Click **OK**.

TIPS

Are there ways to improve the spell check?

Spell check is helpful, but it can miss *contextual errors* — for example, overlooking instances in which the word "there" is used erroneously in lieu of the word "their." To combat this, Outlook includes contextual-spelling capabilities. To enable this feature, click **Tools** and then **Options**; in the Options dialog box's **Spelling** tab, click **Spelling and AutoCorrection**. The Editor Options dialog box appears with the Proofing screen displayed. Under When Correcting Spelling in Outlook, click the **Use Contextual Spelling** check box (●) (☐ changes to ☑).

Are there other proofing tools?

One of the more helpful proofing tools offered by Outlook is its thesaurus, which you can use when you have trouble coming up with just the right word. To do so, right-click the word that is not quite the one you want and choose **Synonyms** in the menu that appears; Outlook lists several possible substitutes. If none of those options suits you, click **Thesaurus** from the menu to display Outlook's Thesaurus feature in the Research pane, where more options are available.

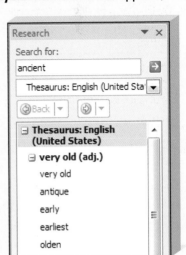

Translate Text

Suppose you need to send an e-mail message to someone who speaks another language — one that you do not speak. Using Outlook's Translate feature, you can convert your message text, written in your own language, into something your recipient can understand.

Languages supported by Outlook's translation feature include French, German, Italian, Spanish, Japanese, Chinese, Russian, and more.

Translate Text

① Compose your message using the language with which you are most familiar.

② Click and drag to select the text you want to translate.

③ Right-click the selected text.

④ Choose **Translate**.

⑤ Choose **Translate**.

● The Research pane opens with the Translation options displayed.

⑥ If necessary, click the **From** ⊡ and select the language in which the message is written.

⑦ Click the **To** ⊡ and choose the language into which the message should be converted (here, **French**).

● Outlook displays the translated text.

⑧ Select the translated text, and right-click it.

⑨ Click **Copy**.

Note: You can close the Research pane by clicking the **Close** button (⊠) in the pane's upper-right corner.

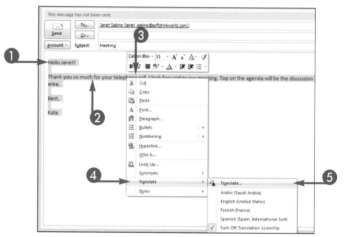

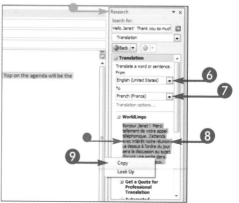

⑩ Right-click the selected message text in the message window. (You might have to reselect it.)

⑪ Click **Paste**.

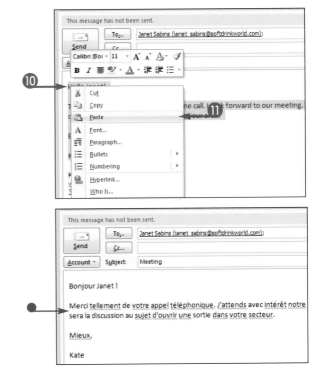

● The translated text is pasted into the body of your message.

This message has not been sent.

To... Janet Sabins (janet_sabins@softdrinkworld.com);
Send Cc...
Account ▾ Subject: Meeting

Bonjour Janet !

Merci tellement de votre appel téléphonique. J'attends avec intérêt notre
sera la discussion au sujet d'ouvrir une sortie dans votre secteur.

Mieux,

Kate

Can I translate messages I receive?

You are not limited to translating messages you send. If you receive a message written in a language you do not understand, you can use Outlook's translation capabilities to translate it into your own language. To do so, right-click the text in the body of the message, click **Translate**, and choose **Translate** again to open the Research pane. Then click the **From** ▾ to choose the language in which the message is written and the language to which it is converted.

What if I do not need to translate the entire message?

If you only need to translate the occasional word, enable Outlook's Translation ScreenTip feature. Right-click in the body of a message (●), click **Translate**, and click the language into which you need to translate; then, simply hover your mouse pointer (🖑) over the word in question. Outlook displays the translated word.

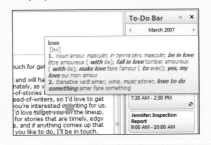

Format
Message Text

You can adjust the text's style, font, size, color, and more to change the look of your message.

You can format text in Outlook in two ways: using the toolbar buttons in the message window's Message Ribbon or using the toolbar buttons found in the Mini toolbar.

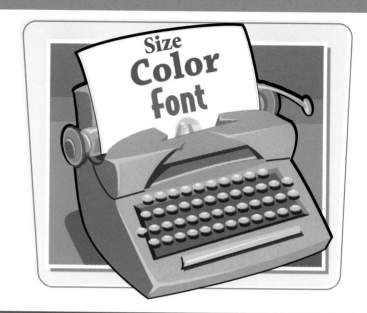

Format Message Text

FORMAT TEXT FROM THE RIBBON

① Compose your message and select the text you want to format.

② Click formatting options.

● Choose a new font.

● Specify a new font size.

To bump your font size up or down, click Ａ or Ａ.

Click ☰ or ☰ to add a bulleted or numbered list.

To clear any formatting applied to the selected text, click ⫶.

③ Click other formatting options.

Apply bold, italics, or underlining by clicking **B**, *I*, and U.

Click to highlight the selected text (ab✓).

To change the color of the text, click Ａ.

Note: *To specify a color other than the one shown, click the down arrow next to* ab✓ *or* Ａ *and choose from the palette that appears.*

Click ☰, ☰, or ☰ to align the text.

Use these buttons to decrease or increase the indent (⫷ or ⫸).

● The format changes are applied.

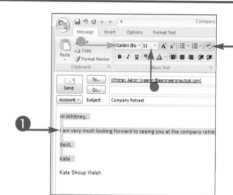

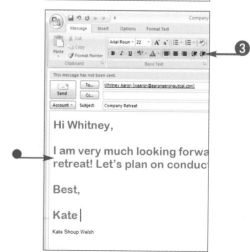

FORMAT TEXT FROM THE MINI TOOLBAR

1️⃣ Compose your message and select the text you want to format.

2️⃣ Place your mouse pointer (↘) over the selected text.

● The Mini toolbar appears.

3️⃣ Click formatting options. (Note that many of the options are identical to those found in the Message Ribbon.)

● Click to apply a different style to the selected text (🅰️).

● Click to access Outlook's Format Painter tool (🖌️), which enables you to copy the formatting of the selected text to other text.

● The format changes are applied.

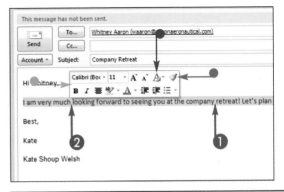

Are there more formatting options?

For more formatting options, click the **Format Text** tab on the message window's Ribbon. In addition to those options covered in this task, you have easy access to styles and other formatting tools.

What happened to the Font dialog box?

You can access the Font dialog box, a holdover from earlier versions of Outlook, by clicking the launcher (🔲) in the Basic Text group of the Message tab.

Use Outlook Stationery and Themes

If you want to spruce up your messages by changing their appearance, you will appreciate Outlook's themes and stationery.

A *theme* is a set of design elements (such as fonts, hyperlink styles, and so on) and color schemes that you can apply to your messages, whereas *stationery* looks like a blank sheet of paper with some sort of design in the background.

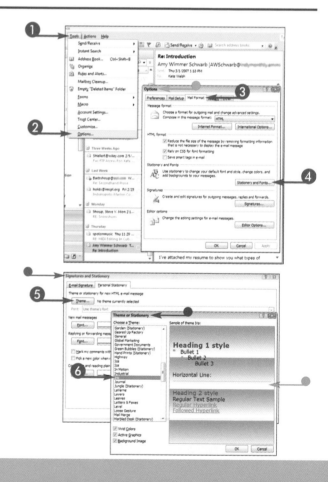

Use Outlook Stationery and Themes

1. Click **Tools**.

2. Click **Options**.

● The Options dialog box appears.

3. Click the **Mail Format** tab.

4. Click **Stationery and Fonts**.

● The Signatures and Stationery dialog box appears with the Personal Stationery tab displayed.

5. Click **Theme**.

● The Theme or Stationery dialog box appears.

6. Click a theme or stationery entry in the Choose a Theme list.

Note: *Stationery entries are indicated by the word "Stationery" in parentheses.*

● A preview of the selected theme or stationery appears.

7 If you opted for a theme rather than stationery, optionally check (or uncheck) any of the following:

Check **Vivid Colors** to enliven the color palette in the selected theme.

If the theme you select supports the use of active graphics (that is, animations), and you want your recipient to be able to see them, check **Active Graphics**.

Check **Background Image** if you want the theme's background image to be displayed (if applicable).

8 Click **OK** to close the Theme or Stationery dialog box.

9 Click **OK** to close the Signatures and Stationery dialog box.

10 Click **OK** to close the Options dialog box.

Messages you create will be employed with the theme or stationery you chose.

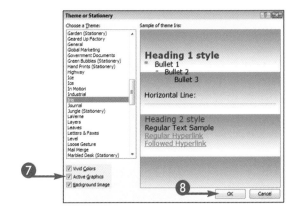

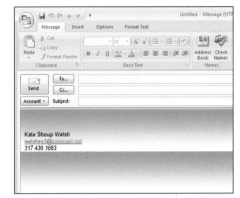

What if I only want to change the font?

Suppose you want to personalize your outgoing messages, but not to the extent of using a theme. One way to do so is to simply change the default font. To do so, click the **Font** button in the Signatures and Stationery dialog box and, in the Font dialog box that appears, select the desired font, size, color, and so on. (Note that you can use separate fonts for new messages; replied and forwarded messages; and plain-text messages.)

Add an E-mail Signature

You can use Outlook to create a signature — that is, a string of text that appears at the bottom of messages you send. This text might include your name, e-mail address, and other contact information; alternatively, it could spell out the name of your business, display a link to your Web site, or even include a picture.

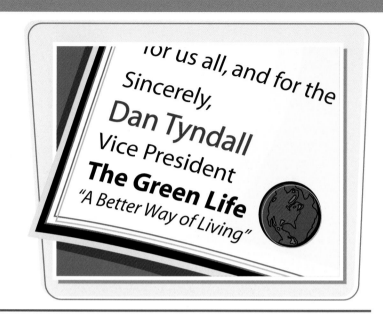

Add an E-mail Signature

① Click **Tools**.

② Click **Options**.

⬤ The Options dialog box appears.

③ Click the **Mail Format** tab.

④ Click **Signatures**.

⬤ The Signatures and Stationery dialog box appears with the E-mail Signature tab displayed.

⑤ Click **New**.

⬤ The New Signature dialog box appears.

⑥ Type a name for the signature you want to create.

⑦ Click **OK**.

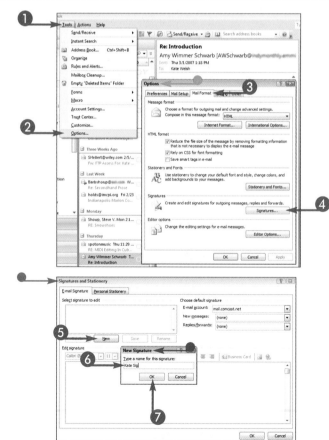

- The new signature's name appears here, selected in the list.

(8) Choose the e-mail account to which the signature should apply.

(9) To include the signature in all outgoing new messages, click the **New Messages** 🔽 and choose the signature from the list.

(10) To include the signature in all replies and forwards, repeat Step **9** with the Replies/Forwards list.

(11) Type the signature text.

(12) Use these controls to format your text.

- Click 🖼 to add a picture to the signature.

- Click 🔗 to insert a hyperlink into the signature.

(13) Click OK.

(14) Click **OK** to close the Options dialog box.

- Messages you create will include the signature you created.

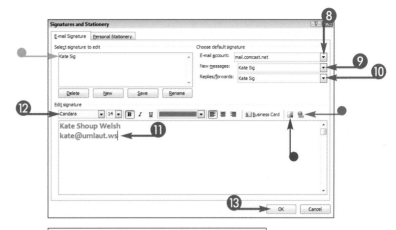

Can I change my signature?

To change your signature, simply open the Signatures and Stationery dialog box, click the signature you want to edit in the list, and make the necessary changes. When you finish, click **OK**.

Can I add an electronic business card to my signature?

To add your electronic business card to your signature, click the **Business Card** button in the Signatures and Stationery dialog box. In the Insert Business Card dialog box, click your contact entry to preview it (●), and click **OK** to add it to your signature.

Use an E-mail Postmark

In an effort to combat spam, Microsoft has introduced e-mail postmarks with Outlook 2007. When added to your message, a postmark communicates to your recipient's computer that your message is legitimate (assuming that computer is configured to process postmarks).

By default, postmarks are enabled. But if the feature is disabled on your machine, enable it by following these steps.

Use an E-mail Postmark

① Click **Tools**.

② Click **Options**.

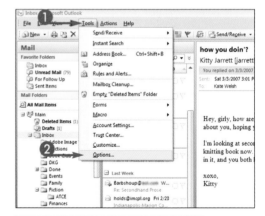

The Options dialog box appears with the Preferences tab displayed.

③ Click **Junk E-mail**.

The Junk E-mail Options dialog box appears.

④ Click the **When Sending E-mail, Postmark the Message** check box (☐ changes to ☑).

⑤ Click **OK** to close the Junk E-mail Options dialog box.

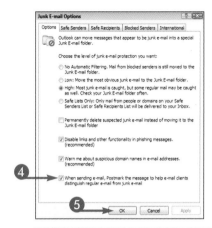

⑥ Click **OK** to close the Options dialog box.

TIP

Can I verify whether my message was received?

If you want verification that your message has been received, you can request a delivery receipt and/or a read receipt. To do so, click the **Options** tab in the message window's Ribbon and click the **Request a Delivery Receipt** and/or **Request a Read Receipt** check boxes (●) (☐ changes to ☑). Then compose and send the message. When your recipient receives and/or reads the message, you receive confirmation.

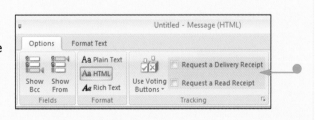

Encrypt a Message

If your message contains highly sensitive information meant for the recipient's eyes only, you can encrypt it. When you encrypt a message, Outlook scrambles the text it contains; only recipients with the necessary "keys" can decipher the message.

To share the necessary keys with the recipient, you must exchange certificates. (A *certificate* is a digital ID.)

Encrypt a Message

ENCRYPT A SINGLE MESSAGE

1 Compose your message.

2 Click the **Options** tab in the message window's Ribbon.

3 Click the launcher (⬚) in the Options tab's Tracking group.

● The Message Options dialog box appears.

4 Click **Security Settings**.

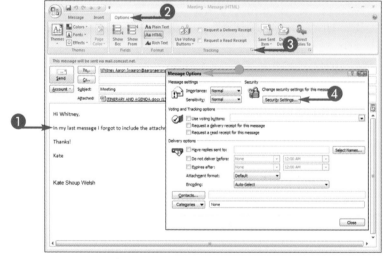

● The Security Properties dialog box appears.

5 Click the **Encrypt Message Contents and Attachments** check box (⬚ changes to ✓).

6 Click **OK** to close the Security Properties dialog box.

7 Click **Close** to close the Message Options dialog box.

ENCRYPT ALL OUTGOING MESSAGES

1 Click **Tools**.

2 Click **Trust Center**.

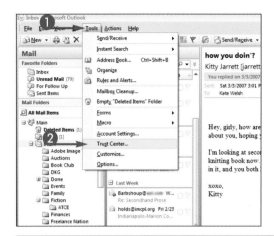

The Trust Center window opens.

3 Click **E-mail Security**.

4 Click the **Encrypt Contents and Attachments for Outgoing Messages** check box (☐ changes to ☑).

5 Click **OK**.

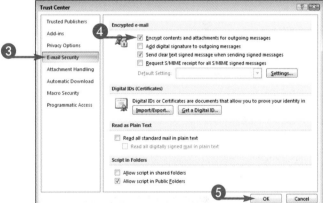

TIPS

How do I obtain a certificate?

To obtain a certificate, or digital ID, click **Get a Digital ID** in the Trust Center's E-mail Security screen. Doing so launches a special Web page with links to several organizations that issue certificates.

How do I exchange certificates?

One way to ensure that the recipient of your encrypted message has the necessary keys is to send a message to him or her that is digitally signed. The recipient can then save your information, including the digital ID, to his or her contacts. To digitally sign e-mail messages, click the **Add Digital Signature to Outgoing Messages** check box (☐ changes to ☑) in the Trust Center's E-mail Security screen.

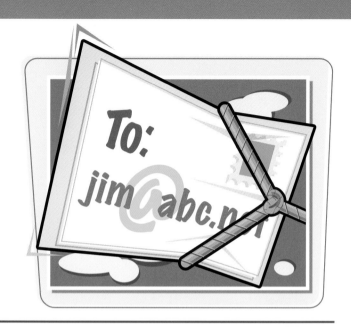

Recall a Message

Suppose after sending your message you realize it contains an error. Assuming the message has not yet been received by the recipient, you may be able to *recall* it.

When you recall a message, Outlook gives you the option of replacing it with an updated version.

Recall a Message

① Click the **Sent Items** folder in the navigation pane.

The message list displays messages you have sent.

② Double-click the message you want to recall.

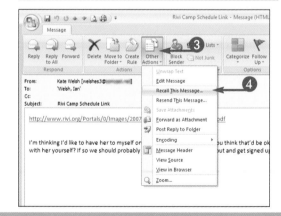

The message opens in its own window.

③ In the Message tab's Actions group, click **Other Actions**.

④ Click **Recall This Message**.

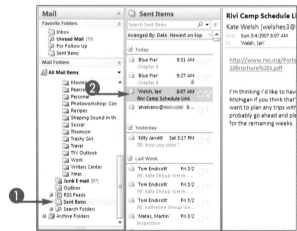

The Recall This Message dialog box appears.

⑤ Click the desired recall option (◎ changes to ◉).

● Click here to delete the message from the recipient's inbox (provided it has not yet been read).

● Click here to delete the unread message from the recipient's inbox and replace it with a new version (selected here).

● If you want Outlook to inform you whether the recall is successful (or not), click this check box (☐ changes to ☑).

⑥ Click **OK**.

⑦ Make the necessary changes to the message and send it.

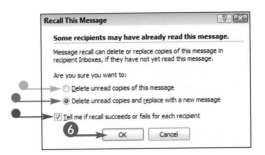

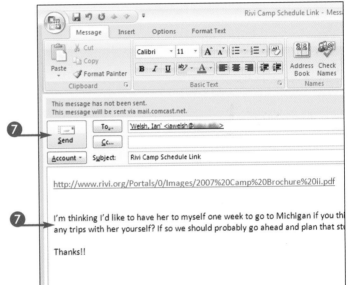

Why did the recall operation not work?

In order to recall or replace a sent message, you and the message's recipient must be using a Microsoft Exchange 2000, 2003, or 2007 account. If your account is a home or personal account, chances are it is probably not an Exchange account.

Is my account a Microsoft Exchange account?

To determine whether your Outlook account is a Microsoft Exchange account, hold down the [Ctrl] key on your keyboard as you right-click the Outlook icon in the notification area in the Windows taskbar; then click Connection Status. The Microsoft Exchange Connection Status window opens, indicating whether you are indeed using an Exchange account.

Set Up an Out-of-Office Reply

Suppose you will not have access to e-mail for a time — for example, if you are on vacation. You can configure Outlook to automatically send an *out-of-office reply* anytime you receive an e-mail during your absence, indicating that you do not have access to your account but will respond to the sender as soon as possible.

Set Up an Out-of-Office Reply

1 In Outlook Mail, click the **New** button.

A new message window opens.

2 Click the **Options** tab.

3 Click **Plain Text**.

4 Type the message you want to include in your out-of-office reply.

5 Click the Microsoft **Office** button.

6 Click **Save As**.

● The Save As dialog box appears, with the contents of the Templates folder displayed.

7 Type a name for this message (**Out of Office Reply** in this example).

8 Click the **Save as Type** and choose **Outlook Template (*.oft)** from the list that appears.

9 Click **Save**.

Note: *If the message window does not close automatically, click its **Close** ([×]) button to close it.*

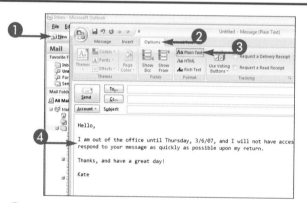

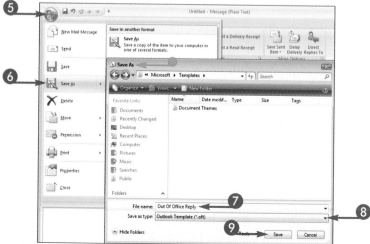

⑩ Click **Tools** to begin creating a rule that uses the message template you just created for the out-of-office replies.

⑪ Click **Rules and Alerts**.

● The Rules and Alerts dialog box appears.

⑫ Click **New Rule**.

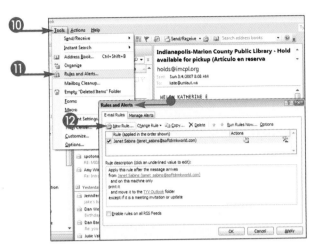

The Rules Wizard opens.

⑬ Under Start from a Blank Rule, click **Check Messages When They Arrive**.

⑭ Click **Next**.

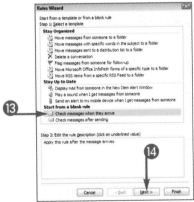

 TIPS

Why did Outlook not send the auto-reply?

In order for Outlook to send your out-of-office reply, your computer must be on with Outlook running. In addition, Outlook must be set up to periodically check for incoming messages.

Are auto-replies sent repeatedly to the same person?

Even if you receive more than one message from a sender while you are away, Outlook sends your out-of-office reply only once — provided the program is not restarted during your absence, in which case it resets the list it keeps of senders to which it has responded.

Auto-reply has been sent to:
Lisa Wynn
Sam Harkness
Colin Nicholls
Rebecca Loos
Carrie Oppenhein
Richard Davies
Davina Tenna
Paul Gerhardt
James Kirkwood

continued

The precise steps for setting up an out-of-office reply differ depending on what type of Outlook account you have. This task outlines how to set up an automatic reply for a POP or IMAP account, a process that involves setting up a message template and then creating a rule that employs that template.

Set Up an Out-of-Office Reply *(continued)*

⑮ In the Rules Wizard's Which Condition(s) Do You Want to Check page, click the **Sent Only to Me** check box (☐ changes to ☑).

⑯ Click **Next**.

⑰ In the Rules Wizard's What Do You Want to Do with the Message page, click the **Reply Using a Specific Template** check box (☐ changes to ☑).

⑱ Click the **A Specific Template** link.

● The Select a Reply Template dialog box appears.

⑲ Click the **Look In** ▾ and choose **User Templates in File System**.

⑳ Click the template you just created to select it.

㉑ Click **Open**.

㉒ Click **Next**.

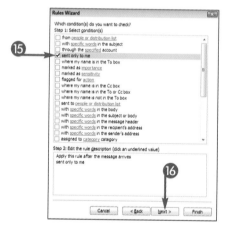

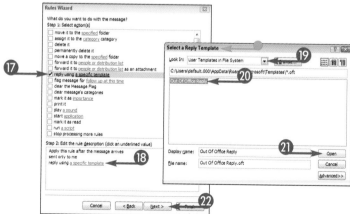

㉓ In the Rules Wizard's Are There Any Exceptions page, click any exceptions you want to apply to the out-of-office reply rule (□ changes to ☑).

㉔ Click **Next**.

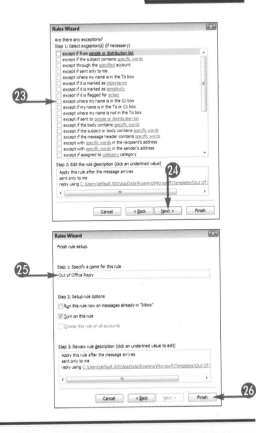

㉕ In the final wizard page, type a name for the rule.

㉖ Click **Finish**.

Outlook applies the rule.

 TIPS

What if I use an Exchange account?

If you use an Exchange account rather than a POP or IMAP account, you follow a different — and, frankly, simpler — series of steps to set up an out-of-office reply. To begin, click **Tools** and then **Out of Office Assistant**; follow the on-screen prompts.

How do I disable the out-of-office reply?

To disable the out-of-office reply, do the following:

① Open the **Tools** menu and click **Rules and Alerts**.

② In the Rules and Alerts dialog box, click the rule that defines the out-of-office reply (□ changes to ☑).

③ Click the **Delete** button.

④ When prompted, confirm the deletion by clicking **OK**.

⑤ Click **OK** to close the Rules and Alerts dialog box.

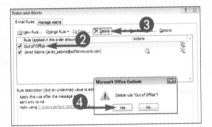

Text Messaging in Outlook

New in Outlook 2007 is Outlook Mobile Service, which works in conjunction with your wireless provider to enable you to create and send text messages to a mobile device. You can also use Outlook to send and receive instant messages with others, enabling you to chat in real time.

Enable Text Messaging in Outlook

You can use Outlook to send and receive instant messages with others, enabling you to chat in real time. In order to do so, however, you must set up an account with an Outlook Mobile Service provider. Microsoft has created a special Web site to help you get started, which you can launch during the setup process.

Enable Text Messaging in Outlook

① Click **Tools**.

② Click **Account Settings**.

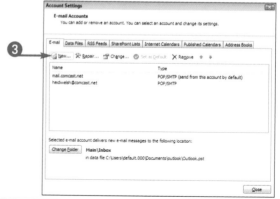

The Account Settings dialog box appears.

③ Click **New**.

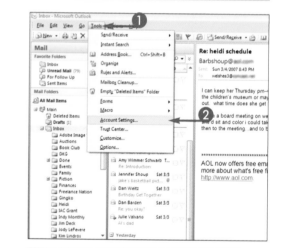

The Add New E-mail Account dialog box appears.

④ Click **Other** (⦿ changes to ⦿).

⑤ Click **Outlook Mobile Service (Text Messaging)**.

⑥ Click **Next**.

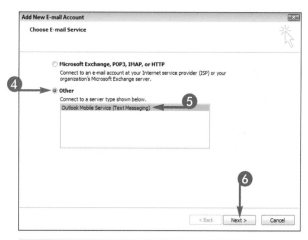

The Add New Outlook Mobile Service Account dialog box appears.

⑦ Click **Fill In This Information Using Microsoft Office Online Configuration**.

 TIPS

How do I change my Mobile Service Account settings?

To edit your Outlook Mobile Service account settings after you create the account, click **Tools**, click **Account Settings**, and, in the Account Settings dialog box, click the Outlook Mobile Service account you want to change and click **Change**. Outlook launches the Change Outlook Mobile Service Account dialog box, where you can adjust the account setting as needed.

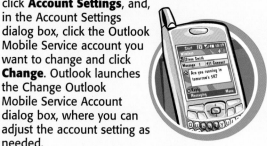

Can I give my Outlook Mobile Service account a more descriptive name?

To rename your Outlook Mobile Service account, click the **More Settings** button in the Change Outlook Mobile Service Account dialog box. Then, in the Outlook Mobile Service Information and Settings dialog box, type a descriptive name for the account in the **Account Name** field (●), and click **OK**.

continued

Enable Text Messaging
in Outlook *(continued)*

When you set up your Outlook
Mobile Service account, it helps to
keep your mobile phone handy. That
is because during the online setup
process, you receive a text message
containing a special code that you
need to type in a setup page.

Enable Text Messaging in Outlook *(continued)*

Windows launches Internet Explorer
and displays Microsoft's Outlook
Mobile Service configuration page.

⑧ Follow the online prompts to set up
your Outlook Mobile Service account.

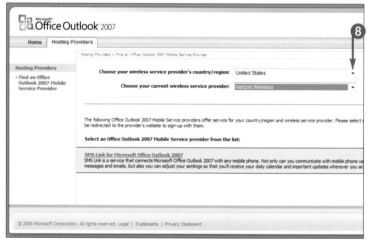

● After you create the account with the
Outlook Mobile Service provider, the
necessary information is automatically
added to the Add New Mobile Services
Account dialog box.

⑨ Click **OK**.

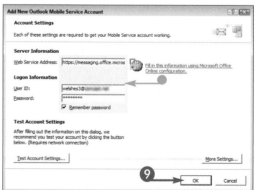

Outlook informs you that you must restart the program.

⑩ Click **OK**.

⑪ Click **File**.

⑫ Click **Exit**.

Outlook closes; restart it as normal.

Can I test my account settings?

Click the **Test Account Settings** button in the Add New Outlook Mobile Service Account dialog box to ensure that everything is as it should be. Outlook tests the settings (●) and informs you of the results (●).

How do I delete an Outlook Mobile Service account?

To delete an Outlook Mobile Service account, click **Tools** and click **Account Settings**. In the Account Settings dialog box, click the Outlook Mobile Service account you want to delete, and click the **Remove** button.

Send a Text Message

If you need to reach someone who is on the go, sending a text message is a great option. You can send text messages from directly within Outlook using your Outlook Mobile Service account.

If someone sends you a text message from a mobile phone, Outlook treats it as it would an incoming e-mail message, delivering it to your inbox.

① Click **File**.

② Click **New**.

③ Click **Text Message**.

Note: If you do not see a Text Message option, it may be because you have not yet set up your Outlook Mobile Service account. Refer to the previous task, "Enable Text Messaging in Outlook," for help.

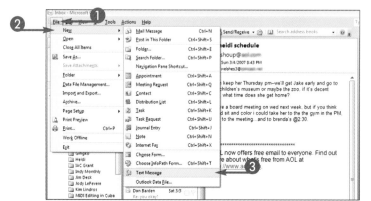

● A new text message window opens.

④ Click **Address Book**.

Note: If you know the recipient's e-mail address or mobile phone number by heart, simply type it in the To field instead of selecting it from the Select Names dialog box.

● The Select Names dialog box appears, listing those entries in Contacts that contain a mobile phone number.

⑤ Click the entry for the text message's recipient.

⑥ Click **To**.

⑦ Click **OK**.

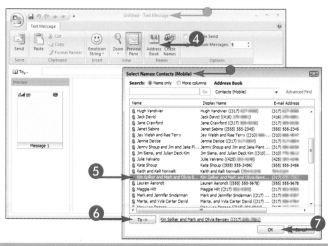

8 Type your message.

● A preview of your message appears here.

9 Click **Send**.

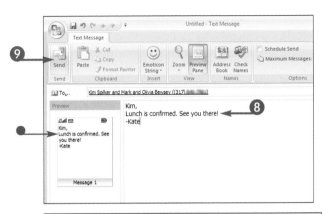

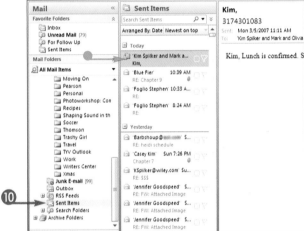

Outlook sends the text message.

10 To verify that the message was sent, click **Sent Items** in the folder list.

● The text message appears in the message list.

What if I do not have time to finish my message?

Just as you can save an e-mail message as a draft, so, too, can you save a text message. To do so, click the **Office** button in the upper-left corner of the text message window and choose **Save** (●). When you are ready to resume work on the text message, access it from the Drafts folder in the folder list.

Can I use emoticons?

Inserting emoticons in a message can help convey to the recipient your true intentions — for example, whether you are sad, angry, or just kidding around. To insert an emoticon into a message, click in the spot where you want it to appear, click **Emoticon String** (●), and select the desired graphic from the list that appears.

Create a Signature for Text Messages

Just as you can add a signature to your e-mail messages, you can also set up a signature for your text messages. That way, when others receive a message from you, they see your contact (or other) info at a glance.

1 Click **Tools**.

2 Click **Options**.

● The Options dialog box appears.

3 Click the **Mail Format** tab.

4 Click **Signatures**.

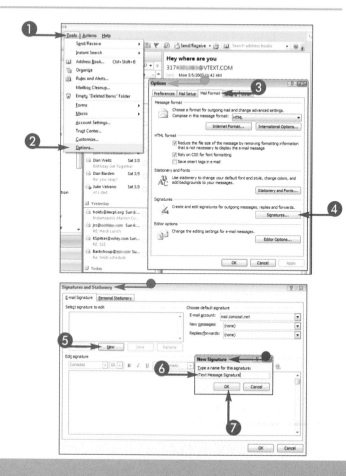

● The Signatures and Stationery dialog box appears, with the E-mail Signature tab displayed.

5 Click **New**.

● The New Signature dialog box appears.

6 Type a name for the new signature.

7 Click **OK**.

132

● The name of the new signature is added to the Select Signature to Edit field.

⑧ Click the new signature to select it.

⑨ Type the signature text.

⑩ Click the **E-mail Account** ⏷ and choose the Outlook Mobile Service account to which you want to apply the signature.

⑪ Click the **New Messages** ⏷ and choose the signature name to add the signature to all new messages.

⑫ Click the **Replies/Forwards** ⏷ and choose the signature name to add the signature to all replies and forwards.

⑬ Click **OK**.

● Outlook adds the signature you created to your text messages.

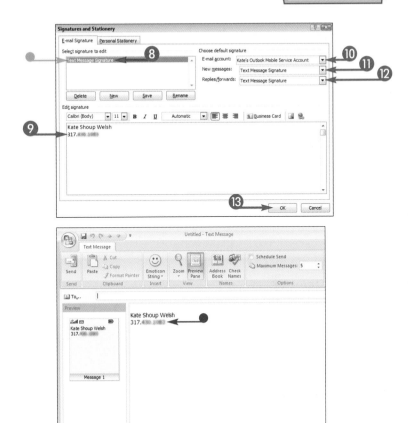

Can I format my signature?

You can format the signature text — for example, change its font, alignment, and so on — using the various buttons above the Edit Signature field. In addition, you can add a picture, a hyperlink, or even an electronic business card to the signature.

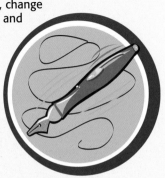

Can I edit my signature?

To change your signature, simply open the Signatures and Stationery dialog box, click the signature you want to edit in the list, and make the necessary changes. When you finish, click **OK**.

Regal MacDonald
Founding Partner
RGM Industries LLC

317-555-1299
1-800-555-REGAL
regal.mac@gmail.com

www.rgm.com/regal

Forward Outlook Information to Your Mobile Device

If you know you will be away from your PC, you can configure Outlook to forward, or *redirect*, Outlook items, including messages, calendar alerts, and more to your mobile device.

As soon as you are back in the office, you can then instruct Outlook to cease forwarding these items to your mobile device.

Forward Outlook Information to Your Mobile Device

1 Click **Tools**.

2 Click **Options**.

3 In the Options dialog box, under Mobile, click **Notifications**.

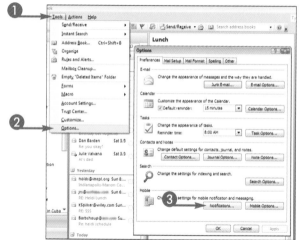

The Outlook Mobile Notification dialog box appears.

4 If the number to which you want to forward messages is different from the one listed, type the correct number here.

5 Select the **Forward Messages that Meet All of the Selected Conditions** check box.

● Select this check box and use the list to specify whether messages sent only to you, with your name in the To box, with your name in the CC box, or all of the above should be forwarded.

● Select this check box to forward messages from certain people only. If you opt to forward messages from certain people only, click **Select** and choose the appropriate contact entries.

● Select this check box to forward messages marked urgent.

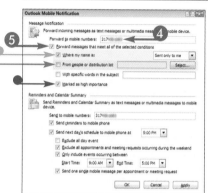

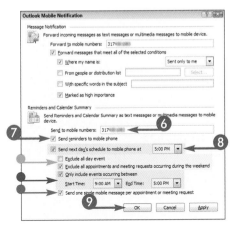

6 If the number to which you want to forward reminders and calendar summaries is different from the one listed, type the correct number here.

7 Select this check box to forward reminders to your mobile phone.

8 Select this check box to send the next day's schedule to your mobile phone, and use the list to specify what time it should be sent.

● Select these check boxes to exclude all-day or weekend events.

● To include appointments within a certain timeframe only, select this check box and use the lists to set start and end times.

● To receive one message per appointment or meeting request, select this check box.

9 Click **OK**.

10 Click **OK**.

Can I change the redirection settings?

One way to change the redirection settings is to simply open the Outlook Mobile Notification dialog box and make the necessary changes. Another is to use the Rules Wizard, because the redirection parameters are, essentially, a rule. To do so, click **Tools**, click **Rules and Alerts**, and, in the E-mail tab of the Rules and Alerts dialog box, click **Change Rule** and choose **Edit Rule Settings** (●) from the drop-down list that appears. The Rules Wizard starts; follow the wizard's on-screen prompts.

How do I configure Outlook to stop forwarding items to my mobile device?

To instruct Outlook to stop redirecting items to your mobile device, simply clear the check boxes in the Outlook Mobile Notification dialog box and click **OK**.

View the Online Status of an IM Contact

If you enjoy instant messaging, you will appreciate Outlook's built-in IM capabilities. Using Outlook, you can chat with others who use Windows Live Messenger, Microsoft Office Communicator, MSN Messenger, and Windows Messenger. In order to chat with someone using IM, you must first determine whether that person is online; first, however, you must enable Outlook to determine a contact's online status.

View the Online Status of an IM Contact

ENABLE ONLINE STATUS CHECKS

1 With a message from your intended recipient displayed in the reading pane, click **Tools**.

2 Click **Options**.

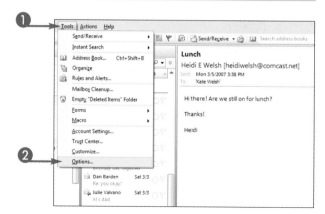

The Options dialog box appears.

3 Click the **Other** tab.

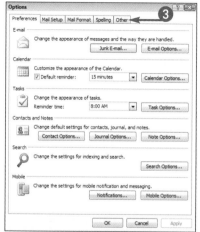

④ Click the **Display Online Status Next to a Person Name** check box (☐ changes to ☑).

⑤ Click **OK**.

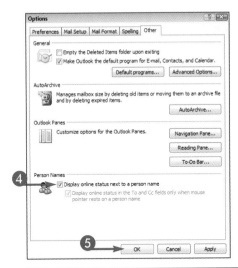

VIEW THE ONLINE STATUS OF AN IM CONTACT

① Place your mouse pointer (👆) over the person's name in the reading pane.

● The person's online status is displayed.

Note: If you have added a contact's instant messaging address to his or her contact record, then you can follow the steps in this task to determine whether he or she is online. The online status for contacts for whom no IM address has been entered cannot be viewed.

TIPS

How do I send an IM to a contact?

Assuming the contact is online, you can send an IM to him or her by right-clicking the status indicator found in a message from the contact or in his or her contact record and choosing **Send Instant Message**. You receive IMs from others in your Outlook inbox, just as you would an e-mail or text message.

How do I update a contact to include IM information?

To add a contact's IM information to Outlook, simply open the contact's record, and type his or her IM address in the record's IM Address field (●). Note that once you add this information, you can see the contact's online status from within his or her contact record.

Using RSS Feeds

Really Simple Syndication (RSS) is a technology that enables Web content to be *syndicated* — that is, converted to a Web feed. This content might include blogs, podcasts, news, and so on. You can use Outlook to subscribe to RSS feeds, in which case Outlook automatically checks for and downloads feed updates. Subscribing to a feed is typically free.

Detect RSS Feeds with a Web Browser

Although you can use Outlook to view feeds to which you have subscribed, you cannot use the program to locate feeds in which you might be interested. For that, you must use a Web browser such as Internet Explorer 7 (shown here), which automatically detects the presence of RSS links.

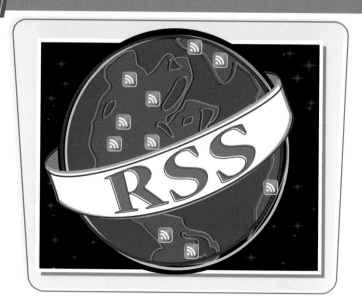

Detect RSS Feeds with a Web Browser

① Click **Start**.

② Click **Internet**.

Internet Explorer 7 opens.

③ Navigate to the Web page of your choice.

If Internet Explorer 7 detects an RSS link, the browser's RSS Feeds button changes from 🔲 to 🔲.

④ Click 🔽 next to the RSS Feeds button and choose the feed you want to view.

A page for the selected feed opens, listing recent feed updates (in this example, articles about travel deals).

⑤ Click a link to one of the feed updates to view it.

Frommers.com Deals & News

You are viewing a feed that contains frequently updated content. When you subscribe to a feed, it is added to the Common Feed List. Updated information from the feed is automatically downloaded to your computer and can be viewed in Internet Explorer and other programs. Learn more about feeds.

⚜ Subscribe to this feed

Vegas, Jr.? Laughlin, Nevada's Gambling, Ghosts and Golf ◀ ⑤

Yesterday, March 06, 2007, 12:00:00 AM | Robert Haru Fisher ➜

The city slickers up in Las Vegas used to turn up their noses at Laughlin, when the little burg tried to lure away visitors from The Strip. But for a place that didn't exist 43 years ago, Laughlin has come a long way, baby.

Ditch the Briefcase, Grab the Snorkel and Explore Taiwan's Great Outdoors

Yesterday, March 06, 2007, 12:00:00 AM | Chans Atlas Heelan ➜

From scuba diving and surfing to ecotourism, birding and wildlife tours, Taiwan is an interesting dichotomy -- both a serious financial and manufacturing center and a outdoor vacation destination.

A page containing the feed update opens.

Frommer's® Travel Experts for **50** YEARS

FREE Newsletters! » Win a FREE Trip! »

Search in... Deals/News ▾ Go

Home | Destinations | Hotels | **Trip Ideas** | Deals & News | Book a Trip | Tips & Tools | Travel Talk | Bookstore

🔊 AIM ✉ Email 🖨 Print ⚡ RSS

Road Trip
▸ Deals & News
▸ Message Boards

Activities
▸ Beach & Water Sports
▸ Cruise
▸ Cultural Immersion
▸ Outdoor & Adventure
▸ Road Trip
▸ Theme Park
▸ Winter Sport

Lifestyles
▸ Disabled
▸ Family
▸ Gay & Lesbian

Vegas, Jr.? Laughlin, Nevada's Gambling, Ghosts & Golf

By Robert Haru Fisher
March 6, 2007

The city slickers up in Las Vegas used to turn up their noses at Laughlin, the town about 80 miles south, when the little burg began to try to lure visitors there and away from The Strip. But for a place that didn't exist 43 years ago, Laughlin has come a long way, baby.

It was back in 1964 that a former Vegas nightclub owner, Don Laughlin, flew over the place and decided to buy a boarded-up motel and six acres on the riverfront in South Pointe, opposite Bullhead City, Arizona, for $250,000. In less than two years, the motel offered all-you-can-eat chicken dinners for 98 cents, 12 slot machines, two live gaming tables and four rooms to sleep in. (The Laughlin family bunked in the property's other four bedrooms.)

Hertz. Fun Collection

$30 OFF WEEKEND RENTALS

TIPS

How can I find RSS feeds?

If you have trouble finding Web sites with feeds that interest you, try using an RSS search site such as www. syndic8.com or www.search4rss. com.

What is the advantage of using feeds?

One chief advantage that feeds provide is that they protect your privacy. That is, rather than requiring you to sign up for, say, an e-mail newsletter, in which case you must provide your name, e-mail address, and other personal information, signing up for an RSS feed is an anonymous process.

PRIVATE

Subscribe to an RSS Feed with a Web Browser

In addition to using a Web browser to detect RSS feeds, you can also use a browser to subscribe to a feed. If the browser you use to subscribe to a feed is Internet Explorer 7, you can automatically access the feed from within Outlook 2007.

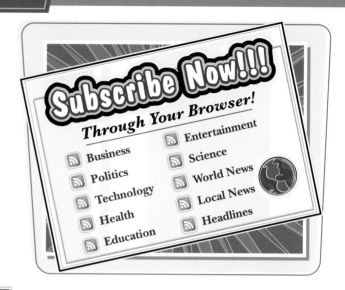

Subscribe to an RSS Feed with a Web Browser

① Click **Start**.

② Click **Internet**.

Internet Explorer 7 opens.

③ Navigate to the Web page containing the feed to which you want to subscribe.

④ Click 🔽 next to the RSS Feeds button and choose the feed to which you want to subscribe.

A page for the selected feed opens, listing recent feed updates.

5 Click **Subscribe to This Feed**.

● An Internet Explorer dialog box appears, displaying information about the feed.

6 Click **Subscribe**.

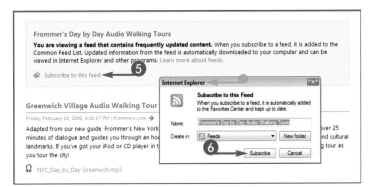

7 In Outlook Mail, double-click the **RSS Feeds** folder in the folder list.

● The feed to which you subscribed is listed.

Why are additional feeds listed in my RSS Feeds folder?

Outlook pre-subscribes you to various feeds automatically. These include the Microsoft at Home feed, the Microsoft at Work feed, and the MSNBC News feed. If you like, you can unsubscribe to any and all of these feeds; to learn how, read the task "Unsubscribe from an RSS Feed" later in this chapter.

Does Microsoft suggest any other feeds?

In Outlook Mail, double-click the **RSS Feeds** folder (●) in the folder list to view a list of suggested feeds. You can find links to feeds from *Forbes Magazine*, FOXsports.com, *Newsweek, Slate Magazine*, and more.

Subscribe to an RSS Feed within Outlook

If you already know the Web address, or URL, of the feed that interests you, you can subscribe to that feed from within Outlook.

When you do, Outlook gives you the option to change certain settings such as how frequently Outlook checks for new posts and whether posts should be downloaded completely or in abstract form.

Subscribe to an RSS Feed within Outlook

① Click **Tools** in Outlook.

② Click **Account Settings**.

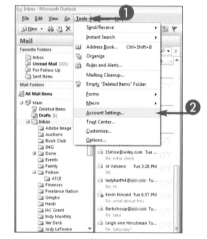

● The Account Settings dialog box appears.

③ Click the **RSS Feeds** tab.

④ Click **New**.

● The New RSS Feed dialog box appears.

⑤ Type the URL for the feed to which you want to subscribe.

⑥ Click **Add**.

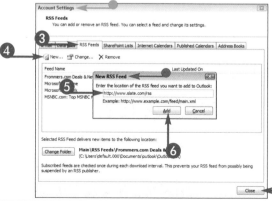

- In the RSS Feed Options dialog box, the name of the feed appears here.

- To change the folder in which feed updates are saved, click here and select the desired folder.

- Click here to automatically download feed enclosures.

- Click here to download entire feed articles rather than abstracts.

- The publisher of the feed to which you are subscribing likely limits how frequently you can check for new postings. Select this check box to ensure Outlook does not check more frequently than is permitted.

⑦ Click **OK**.

⑧ Click **Close** in the Account Settings dialog box.

⑨ In Outlook Mail, double-click the **RSS Feeds** folder in the folder list.

- The feed to which you subscribed is listed.

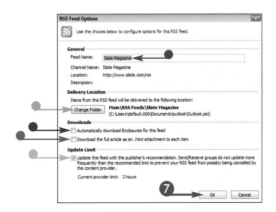

TIPS

What is an enclosure?

An *enclosure* is a link within an RSS feed post that you can click to access a file or Web page. If you opt to automatically download feed enclosures as described in this task, then Outlook goes ahead and pulls the file or page to which the link attaches rather than requiring you to click the link in order to access the file or page.

Can I check for new posts automatically?

If you do not want to wait for Outlook to run its automatic check for new posts, you can check manually. To do so, do the following:

① In the folder list, click the folder for the RSS feed you want to check.

② Click one of the posts in the message list to display the post's contents in the reading pane.

③ Click the Info Bar at the top of the post in the reading pane.

④ Click **Download/ Update All Content**.

Subscribe to a Shared Feed

Suppose someone you know subscribes to a feed that interests you. If that person also uses Outlook 2007, he or she can share that feed with you via e-mail. When someone shares a feed in this way, subscribing to the feed is as simple as clicking a button.

Subscribe to a Shared Feed

① When someone shares a feed with you via e-mail, double-click the message containing the feed in the message list.

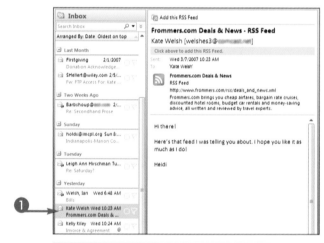

The message with the feed opens in its own window.

● Information about the shared feed appears here.

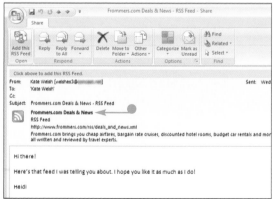

② Click **Add this RSS Feed**.

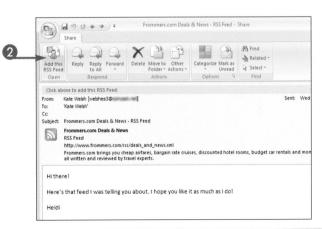

Outlook subscribes to the feed.

③ To verify that you have subscribed to the feed, double-click the **RSS Feeds** folder in the folder list.

● The feed appears in the list.

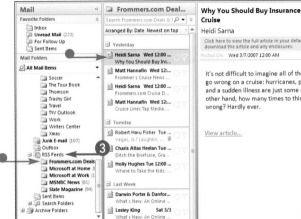

Can I share one of my feeds with someone else?

Just as others can share their feeds with you, you can share your feeds with others. You learn how in the task "Share an RSS Feed" later in this chapter.

Is there a quick way to share multiple feeds?

If someone you know subscribes to several feeds that interest you, he or she can export a special file containing the feeds, which you can import into your PC to automatically subscribe. You learn how in the next task, "Import Feeds."

Import Feeds

If someone exports feeds to an Outline Processor Markup Language (OPML) file and e-mails it to you, you can use the Import and Export Wizard to import those feeds to your PC, meaning you do not need to subscribe to each feed individually.

Import Feeds

1. In Outlook, click **File**.

2. Click **Import and Export**.

   ● The Import and Export Wizard starts.

3. Click **Import RSS Feeds from an OPML File**.

4. Click **Next**.

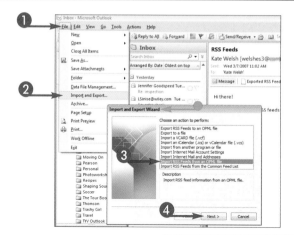

5. In the next screen of the wizard, click **Browse**.

   ● The OPML File dialog box appears.

6. Locate and click the folder in which you saved the OPML file.

7. Click the OPML file to select it.

8. Click **Open**.

9. Click **Next**.

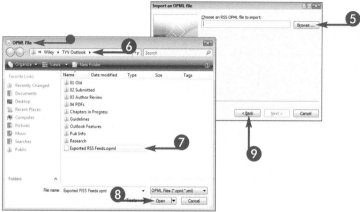

The wizard displays a list of RSS feeds contained in the OPML file.

⑩ Click the check box next to each feed you want to import (☐ changes to ☑).

⑪ Click **Next**.

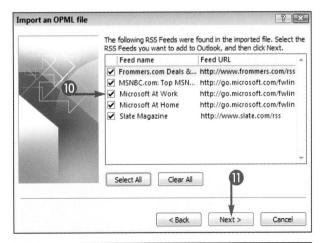

Outlook imports the selected feeds.

⑫ Click **Finish**.

Where is the OPML file located?

Before you run the Import and Export Wizard, first save the OPML file that is attached to the e-mail message you receive from your contact. To do so, do the following:

① Open the message containing the OPML file.

② Right-click the file attachment.

③ Click **Save As**.

④ In the Save Attachment dialog box that appears, locate and select the folder in which you want to save the OPML file.

⑤ Click **Save**.

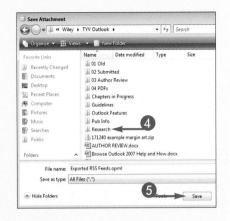

View a Feed Post

When you subscribe to feeds provided by your favorite Web sites, such as news sites or blogs, Outlook automatically downloads to new posts from those feeds. That means that rather than visiting several Web sites to stay informed, you can simply view these various feed posts in Outlook.

View an RSS Feed

1 In Outlook Mail, double-click the **RSS Feeds** folder in the folder list.

2 Click the folder for the feed whose posts you want to read.

The feed's posts appear in the message list.

3 Double-click a post that interests you.

A summary of the post opens in its own window.

④ Read the summary of the post.

⑤ If the summary intrigues you, click the link in the message window to view the post in its entirety.

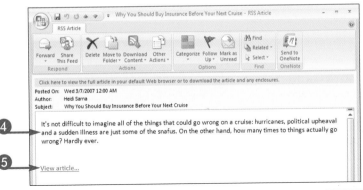

Outlook launches a Web browser and displays the post in its entirety.

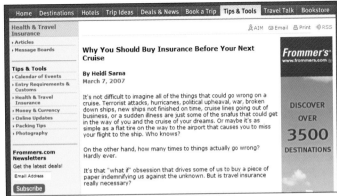

TIPS

Can I print a post?

You can print a post in the same way you print an e-mail message. For more information, refer to the task "Print an E-mail Message" in Chapter 4.

Can I reply to a post?

Although you can forward, delete, and even flag an RSS post, you cannot reply to one.

Download Enclosures as Attachments

Many feeds include enclosures — for example, a link to a Web page that contains more information. One way to access the enclosure is to click the link, as you did in the previous task, "View a Feed Post." Another is to set up Outlook to automatically download any enclosures for you, presenting them as attachments.

Download Enclosures as Attachments

① Click **Tools**.

② Click **Account Settings**.

The Account Settings dialog box appears.

③ Click the **RSS Feeds** tab.

④ Click the RSS feed whose enclosures you want to download automatically.

⑤ Click **Change**.

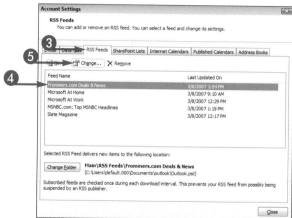

The RSS Feed Options dialog box appears.

⑥ Click the **Download the Full Article as an HTML Attachment to Each Item** check box (☐ changes to ☑).

⑦ Click **OK** to close the RSS Feed Options dialog box.

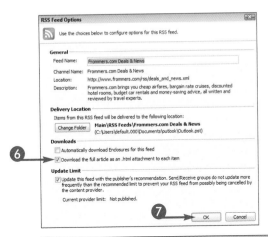

⑧ Click **Close** to close the Account Settings dialog box.

Outlook applies your settings.

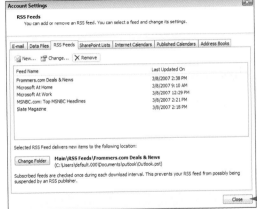

TIPS

How do I open the enclosure?

You open the enclosure just as you would any other attachment: by right-clicking the attachment and clicking **Open** in the menu that appears. Alternatively, save the enclosure by right-clicking it, clicking **Save As**, and, in the Save Attachment dialog box, locating and selecting the folder in which you want to save the enclosure and clicking **Save**.

Can I download enclosures automatically?

If you do not want to have to click a link or open an attachment to view an enclosure, you can configure Outlook to download enclosures automatically. To do so, repeat the steps in this task, but for Step **6**, check the **Automatically Download Enclosures for This Feed** check box in the RSS Feed Options dialog box (☐ changes to ☑).

Share an RSS Feed

Just as others can share an RSS feed with you, you can share a favorite RSS feed with others. When you share a feed, your contact can subscribe to it with the click of a button.

Share an RSS Feed

① In Outlook Mail, double-click the **RSS Feeds** folder in the folder list.

② Click the folder for the RSS feed you want to share.

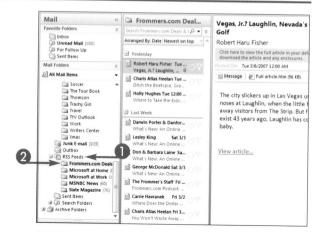

● Outlook displays posts from the feed in the message list.

③ Double-click any of the posts in the message list.

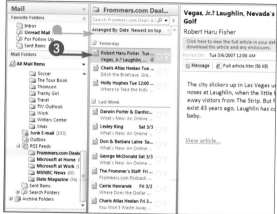

The post opens in its own window.

④ Click **Share this Feed**.

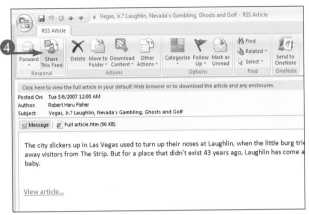

● Outlook launches a new message window with information about the feed embedded in it and a subject entered.

⑤ Type the recipient's address.

⑥ Compose your message.

⑦ Click **Send**.

Outlook sends the RSS feed to the recipient.

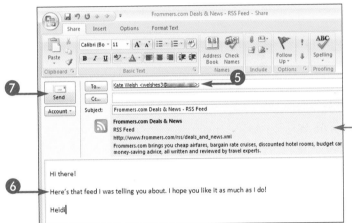

 TIPS

Is there a faster way to share a feed?

Another way to share a feed is to right-click a post from the feed in the message list and click **Share This Feed** in the menu that appears (●).

Can I share a feed via text message?

Although you cannot share a feed via text message, you can forward a post to a mobile device. To do so, right-click a post from the feed in the message list and click **Forward as Text Message** in the menu that appears.

Export a Group of Feeds

If one of your contacts wants to subscribe to all the feeds you do, you can export those feeds as a group, which your contact can then import.

Alternatively, you might export your feeds to back them up on a hard drive; that way, if disaster strikes your computer or you decide to upgrade, you can import the exported group.

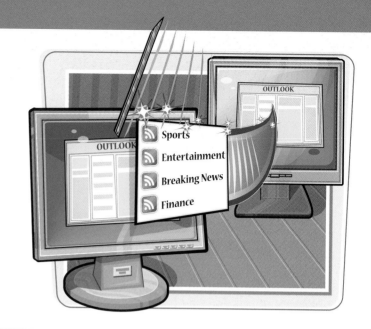

Export a Group of Feeds

① In Outlook Mail, click **File**.

② Click **Import and Export**.

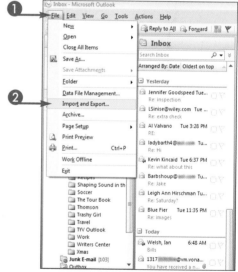

● The Import and Export Wizard starts.

③ Click **Export RSS Feeds to an OPML File**.

④ Click **Next**.

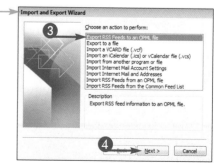

5 Click the check box next to each feed you want to export (☐ changes to ☑).

6 Click **Next**.

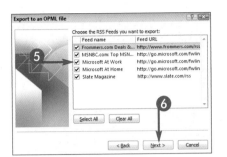

7 In the next screen of the wizard, click **Browse**.

● The OPML File dialog box appears.

8 Locate and select the folder in which you want to save the exported file.

9 Type a descriptive name for the exported file.

10 Click **Save**.

11 Click **Next**.

Outlook creates and saves the OPML file in the location you specified.

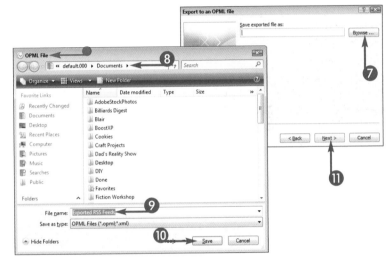

 TIPS

How do I share the exported file?

You can send the exported file to someone else as an e-mail attachment. For more information about sending attachments, see the task "Attach a File" in Chapter 5.

What if my contact does not want to subscribe to all my feeds?

If your contact wants to subscribe to only some of your feeds, simply leave the unwanted feeds unchecked in Step **5**. Alternatively, your contact can opt out of subscribing to unwanted feeds during the import operation.

Unsubscribe from a Feed

You may find that a particular feed is not as interesting or useful as you would like. To prevent Outlook from wasting resources by downloading and storing posts from this feed, you can unsubscribe from it.

Unsubscribe from a Feed

DELETE THE FEED AND ALL DOWNLOADED POSTS

1 Double-click the **RSS Feeds** folder in the folder list.

2 Right-click the folder for the feed you want to remove.

3 Click **Delete *name of feed*** in the menu that appears.

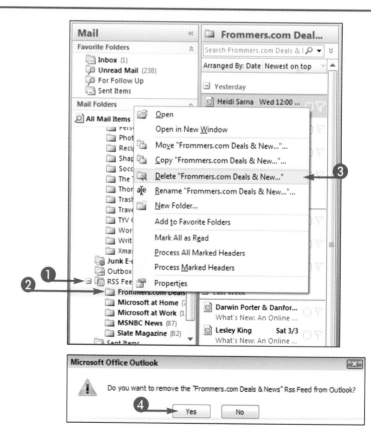

Outlook prompts you to confirm the deletion.

4 Click **Yes**.

Outlook removes the feed and deletes all downloaded posts.

**DELETE THE FEED BUT RETAIN ALL
DOWNLOADED POSTS**

1 Click **Tools**.

2 Click **Account Settings**.

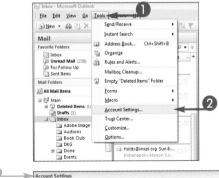

● The Account Settings dialog box appears.

3 Click the **RSS Feeds** tab.

4 Click the feed you want to remove.

5 Click **Remove**.

● Outlook prompts you to confirm the
deletion.

6 Click **Yes**.

7 Click **Close**.

Outlook removes the feed but leaves all
downloaded posts intact.

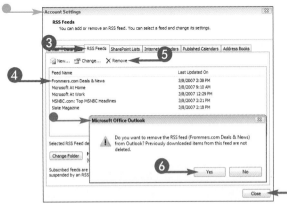

Can I customize my feed?
If you do not want to delete your feed but you do want to
change certain things about it, such as the folder in which
feeds are stored, or the name of the feed as it is displayed
in Outlook, perform the steps that follow. Click **Tools**. Click
Account Settings. In the Account Settings dialog box, click
the **RSS Feeds** tab. Click the feed you want to customize.
Click **Change**. In the RSS Feed Options dialog box, adjust
various feed-related settings as desired (●) and click **OK**.
Click **Close** in the Account Settings dialog box.

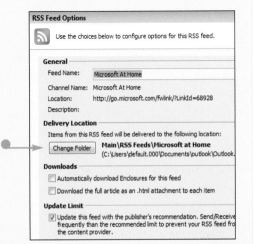

Using the Outlook Calendar

Lunch w/Barry
12:30
at Bistro Paris

Outlook Calendar enables you to schedule one-time events (such as a meeting) or recurring appointments (such as a standing lunch date), and can be configured to send you a reminder about any calendar entries. You can maintain multiple calendars — for example, one for work and one for home — and you can share your calendar with others.

You can display your calendar in Day, Week, or Month view. Day view shows the entries for a single day, with the current day displayed by default. In Week view, you can display entries for the workweek only or for the full seven-day week. In Month view, the entire month is displayed.

Switch Calendar Views

① If Outlook is not yet in Calendar mode, click the Calendar button in the navigation pane.

The Calendar opens in whatever view was displayed the last time you used it.

② To switch views – in this case, from Day to Week – click **Week**.

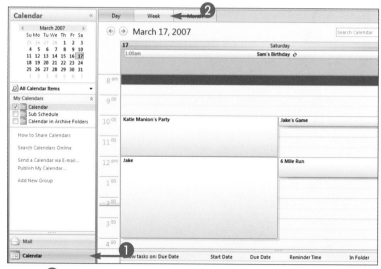

Calendar switches to Week view.

● Select **Show Work Week** to view entries during the workweek only.

● Select **Show Full Week** to view the entire seven-day week.

● Notice how today's date is highlighted.

● Click the right or left arrow to display Calendar entries for the next or previous week, respectively.

③ To switch to Month view, click **Month**.

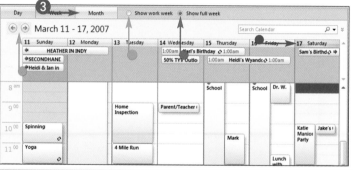

● Select **Low** to view Calendar events (that is, all-day items without a specific start or end time), but not appointments or meetings.

● Select **Medium** to view events and appointments, but with minimal information about each.

● Select **High** to view events and appointments, including appointments' start times, subjects, and locations.

Note: *Be aware that if you have many appointments scheduled on a particular day, Calendar may not have room to display them all in High view.*

● Today's date is highlighted.

● Click the right or left arrow to display Calendar entries for the next or previous week, respectively.

④ To switch back to Day view, click **Day**.

Calendar switches to Day view.

● Click the right or left arrow to display Calendar entries for the next or previous day, respectively.

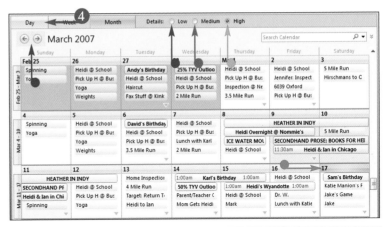

TIPS

Can I jump to another date?
To quickly jump from one date to another, click the desired date in the navigation bar's date navigator. If the date to which you want to jump is in a different month, click the arrow (●) in the upper-left or upper-right corner of the date navigator to locate the desired month.

Can I view multiple time zones?
To display a second time zone in your calendar — helpful if, for example, you have relatives in another part of the world — click **Tools**, click **Options**, and, in the Options dialog box, click **Calendar Options**. In the dialog box that appears, click **Time Zone**; in the Time Zone dialog box, click **Show an Additional Time Zone** (☐ changes to ☑), type a name for the second time zone, click the time zone you want displayed, and, if applicable, click **Adjust for Daylight Saving Time** (☐ changes to ☑).

Change Your Calendar's Appearance

If you do not care for Calendar's default background color or font, you can change them to suit your taste. By default, Outlook Calendar's background color is blue, and the font used is 8 pt. Segoe UI.

Change Your Calendar's Appearance

CHANGE THE BACKGROUND COLOR

1. With Outlook Calendar open, click **Tools**.

2. Click **Options**.

● The Options dialog box appears, with the Preferences tab displayed.

3. Click **Calendar Options**.

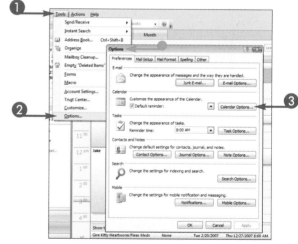

The Calendar Options dialog box appears.

4. Click the **Default Color** ▾.

5. Choose the desired color from the list that appears.

6. Click **OK** to close the Calendar Options dialog box.

7. Click **OK** to close the Options dialog box.

Calendar's background color changes.

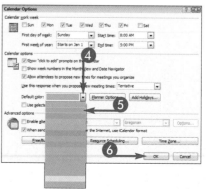

CHANGE THE FONT

1. Click **Tools**.

2. Click **Options**.

● The Options dialog box appears, with the Preferences tab displayed.

3. Click the **Other** tab.

4. Click **Advanced Options**.

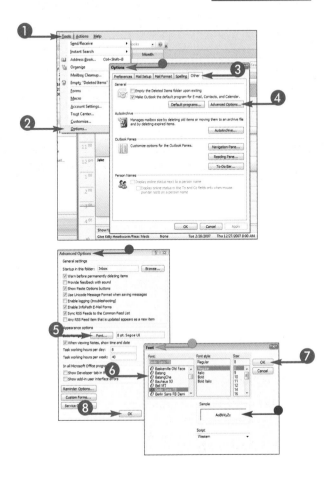

● The Advanced Options dialog box appears.

5. Click **Font**.

● The Font dialog box appears.

6. Make changes to the font, font style, and font size.

● Outlook displays a preview of the font.

7. Click **OK** to close the Font dialog box.

8. Click **OK** to close the Advanced Options dialog box.

9. Click **OK** to close the Options dialog box.

Calendar's font changes.

TIPS

Can I change the time increments?

By default, appointments can be entered in 30-minute increments. You can, however, change the increment to any of the following: 60, 15, 10, 6, or 5 minutes. To do so, right-click anywhere in the Time column (that is, the area of the Calendar where times appear) and choose the desired increment.

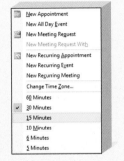

Can I display week numbers?

If you want to be able to view weeks by number while in Month view, you can easily customize Calendar to display them. To do so, click **Tools**, click **Options**, and, in the dialog box that opens, click **Calendar Options**. In the Calendar Options dialog box that appears, click the **Show Week Numbers in the Month View and Date Navigator** check box (☐ changes to ☑).

Schedule an Appointment

Outlook's Calendar function enables you to plan your days by entering *appointments* — events that do not involve inviting others or reserving resources. Appointments can be one-time events, such as a luncheon, or recurring — for example, a weekly meeting. Outlook sends you a reminder about your appointment 15 minutes before it starts (although you can disable or change the default reminder time).

Schedule an Appointment

① In the date navigator, click the date on which the appointment is to occur.

② Click the **New** button.

③ In the new appointment window, type a description.

④ Type the address or other location-related information.

● The Start time and End time entries match the date you selected in Step **1**.

⑤ Click ⏷ to set the appointment's start and end times.

● For an all-day appointment, select **All Day Event** in lieu of setting start and end times.

⑥ Type any notes for the appointment.

● To change the reminder settings, click ⏷ to the right of the **Reminder** button (🔔) and choose the reminder time increment.

⑦ If the appointment is recurring, click the **Recurrence** button.

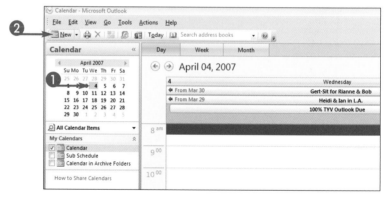

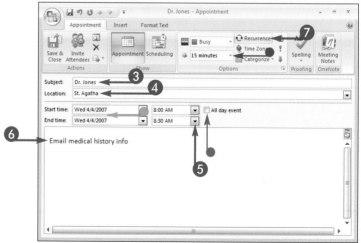

● The Appointment Recurrence dialog box appears.

⑧ Under Recurrence Pattern, select **Daily**, **Weekly**, **Monthly**, or **Yearly**.

⑨ Further define the recurrence pattern. Note that the options here will differ depending on your selection in Step **8**.

⑩ Set the range of recurrence by specifying when the recurrence pattern should end.

⑪ Click **OK**.

⑫ Click **Save & Close**.

● The appointment is added to Calendar. Note the recurring entries.

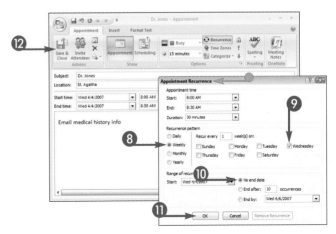

Is there a quicker way to add an appointment?

You can bypass the new appointment window and instead enter an appointment directly into Calendar. To do so, switch to Day view, select the date on which the appointment should occur, click the desired time, type the necessary information, and press Enter. If the appointment will span more than a single time increment, click and drag the edge of the appointment entry to the desired end time.

What if the appointment is private?

If you share your calendar with others, but do not want others to be able to see details about an appointment (or, for that matter, an event or a meeting), you can mark it as private. To do so, click the **Private** button (🔒) in the new meeting window's Options group.

Schedule an Event

Although adding an event to Calendar is similar to adding an appointment, events differ from appointments in that they typically occur once, and they last 24 hours or longer. Examples of events might include trade shows or vacations. Instead of appearing in Calendar as blocks of time, events are displayed as banners along the top of the date entry.

Schedule an Event

① With Calendar open, click **Actions**.

② Click **New All Day Event**.

A new event window opens.

● The All Day Event check box is checked for you.

③ Type a description of the event.

④ Type the event's location.

⑤ Click 🔽 to set the appointment's start and end dates.

⑥ Type any notes pertaining to the event.

● To change the reminder settings, click 🔽 to the right of the **Reminder** button (🔔) and choose the reminder time increment.

⑦ Although events are typically one-time affairs, they can be recurring. If your event is recurring, click the **Recurrence** button.

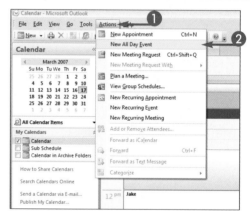

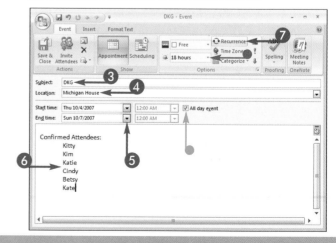

● The Appointment Recurrence dialog box appears.

⑧ Under Recurrence Pattern, click **Daily**, **Weekly**, **Monthly**, or **Yearly** (◯ changes to ◉).

⑨ Further define the recurrence pattern (☐ changes to ☑). Note that the options here differ depending on your selection in Step **8**.

⑩ Set the range of recurrence by specifying when the recurrence pattern should end (◯ changes to ◉).

⑪ Click **OK**.

⑫ Click **Save & Close**.

● The event is added to Calendar.

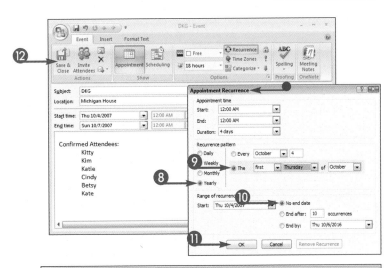

TIPS

Is there a quicker way to add an event?

You can bypass the new event window and instead enter an event directly into Calendar. To do so, switch to Day or Week view, double-click the colored area at the top of the date entry, type the necessary information, and press Enter. If the event spans multiple days, click and drag the edge of the event entry to the desired end date.

Can I add holidays as events?

To add standard holidays to Calendar, click **Tools**, click **Options**, and in the dialog box that appears, click **Calendar Options**. The Calendar Options dialog box appears; click **Add Holidays** and, in the dialog box that appears, click the check box (☐ changes to ☑) next to the country or region whose holidays you want to add (●).

Plan a Meeting

You can use Outlook to plan a meeting — that is, an appointment to which others are invited or for which resources are required — first determining when the attendees will be free and then sending meeting requests to those attendees via e-mail. Invitees can then accept or decline the meeting request, and possibly propose an alternative meeting time.

Plan a Meeting

① With Calendar open, click **File**.

② Click **New**.

③ Click **Meeting Request**.

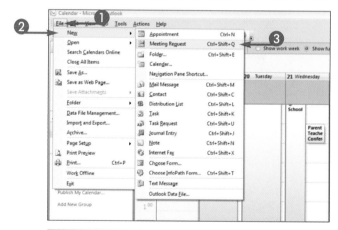

A new meeting window opens.

④ In the new meeting window, type a description.

⑤ Type the event's location.

Note: *If your organization uses Microsoft Exchange Server, you may have the option of reserving the room you want to use for you meeting by clicking a **Rooms** button and selecting the desired room.*

⑥ Click ▾ to set the appointment's start and end dates and times.

⑦ Type any notes for the meeting.

⑧ To include the e-mail addresses of your invitees, click **To**.

Note: *If you know the invitees' e-mail addresses, you can simply type them directly into the To field.*

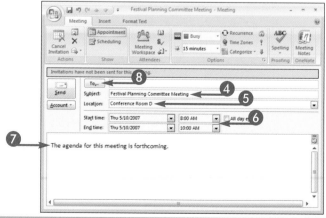

⑨ In the Select Attendees and Resources dialog box, click an invitee.

⑩ If the invitee's attendance is required, click **Required**. If not, click **Optional**.

⑪ Repeat Steps **9** and **10** to add more invitees.

⑫ When all invitees have been added, click **OK**.

The invitees you selected appear in the new meeting window's To field.

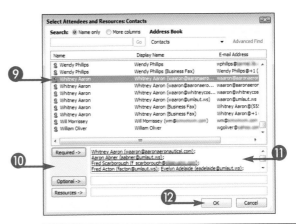

⑬ Click **Scheduling**.

● If you are authorized to view the invitees' calendars, information about their schedules during the proposed meeting time appears.

● If any invitees are listed as busy during the proposed meeting time, click **AutoPick Next** to view the first possible time when all invitees are available.

⑭ When you find a time when all invitees are available, click **Send** to e-mail invitations to the meeting.

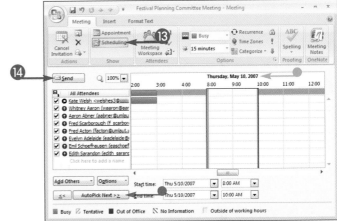

TIPS

How do I track which invitees can attend?

Invitees have the option of accepting, tentatively accepting, or declining your meeting request. They can also propose a different meeting time. To track the status of each invitee, simply double-click the meeting entry in your calendar and click the **Tracking** button that appears in the Meeting tab's Show group.

What if I receive a meeting request from someone else?

If you receive an e-mail containing a meeting request from someone else, open the e-mail, and click **Accept**, **Tentative**, or **Decline** in the Message tab's Respond group. Alternatively, click the **Propose New Time** button, specify whether you are tentatively planning to attend at the current time but proposing a new time or declining to attend at the current time and proposing a new time, and then select a time at which all invitees are available. Finally, click **Propose Time** and click **Send**.

Attach a File to a Calendar Entry

Suppose you have created a Calendar entry for a trade show. You might attach the document containing your travel itinerary for the trade show to the appointment for quick retrieval. Fortunately, Outlook makes it easy to attach files to Calendar events, be they appointments, events, or meetings.

Attach a File to a Calendar Entry

① Create an appointment, event, or meeting.

② Click the **Insert** tab in the new Calendar entry window.

Outlook displays the Ribbon's Insert tab.

③ Click **Attach File**.

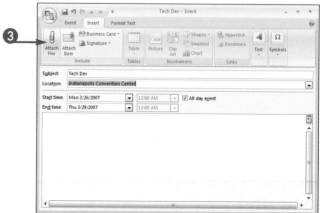

The Insert File dialog box appears.

④ Locate and click the file you want to attach to the Calendar entry.

⑤ Click **Insert**.

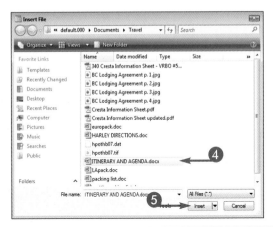

● The file is attached to the Calendar entry.

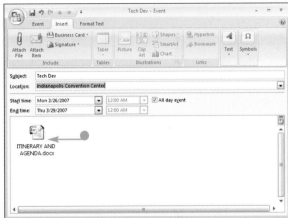

 TIPS

How do I open the attached file?

To open a file attached to a Calendar entry, simply double-click it in the entry.

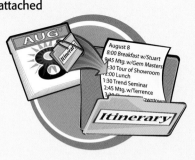

Can I attach an Outlook item to a Calendar entry?

In addition to attaching a file such as a Word document or image file to a Calendar entry, you can also attach Outlook items, such as e-mail messages, Contact entries, and even other Calendar entries. To do so, click **Attach Item** in the Calendar entry's Insert tab. In the Insert Item dialog box, locate and click the Outlook item you want to attach (●), and click **OK**.

Open a Calendar Entry

You can view details about an appointment, event, or meeting when you open it in its own window. When you do, you see any particulars you added when the appointment was added, as well as any subsequent changes. (You learn how to edit an appointment, event, or meeting in the next task.)

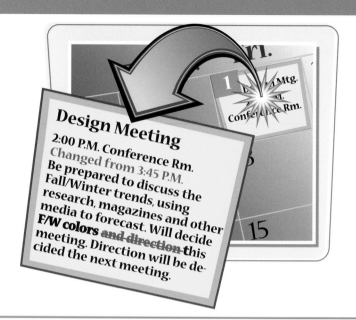

Design Meeting
2:00 P.M. Conference Rm.
Changed from 3:45 P.M.
Be prepared to discuss the Fall/Winter trends, using research, magazines and other media to forecast. Will decide F/W colors and direction this meeting. Direction will be decided the next meeting.

Open a Calendar Entry

① With Calendar open, click the date containing the entry you want to open in the date navigator.

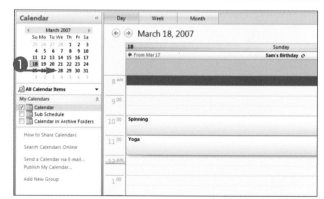

● Calendar displays the day you selected.

② Double-click the entry you want to open.

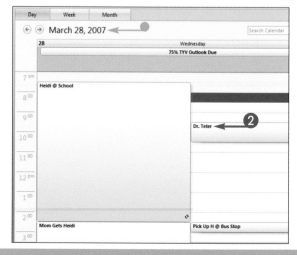

The entry opens in its own window.

③ If Outlook notes that the entry conflicts with other Calendar entries, click **Scheduling**.

Information about other events scheduled at the same time as the open Calendar entry appears.

④ Click the **Close** button (⊠) to close the window for the Calendar entry.

The window closes.

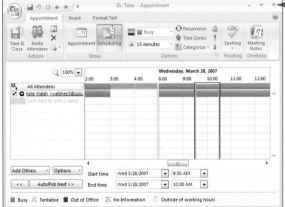

 TIP

What if I cannot find the Calendar event I want to open?

You can use Outlook's Instant Search feature to quickly locate the Calendar event you want to open. To do so, type a keyword you know appears in the Calendar entry in the Search field found in the upper-right corner of Calendar (●); Calendar locates and displays all entries that contain the keyword you typed. When you locate the entry you seek in the list of matching entries, double-click it to open it in its own window.

	Subject	Location	Start	End
	Jake's Birthday Party		Sat 11/11/2006 12...	Sat 11/11/2006 1:...
	Hettie Egan's Birthday		Sun 1/28/2007 2:0...	Sun 1/28/2007 4:0...
Recurrence: Yearly (44 items)				
	Sol Blickman's Birthday		Wed 12/28/1921 1...	Thu 12/29/1921 1...
	Betsy's Birthday		Mon 9/9/2002 1:0...	Tue 9/10/2002 1:0...
	Heidi's Birthday		Thu 9/19/2002 1:0...	Fri 9/20/2002 1:00...
	Jake's Birthday		Wed 11/13/2002 1...	Thu 11/14/2002 1...
	Sally's Birthday		Thu 11/14/2002 1...	Fri 11/15/2002 12:...
	Jay's Birthday		Thu 11/21/2002 1...	Fri 11/22/2002 12:...
	Katie's Birthday		Wed 11/27/2002 1...	Thu 11/28/2002 1...

Calendar (Search Results) — Birthday

Edit a Calendar Entry

Outlook makes it easy to add to or otherwise change the information in a Calendar appointment, event, or meeting. Simply open the entry and use the tools available in the entry's window to make the necessary changes.

Edit a Calendar Entry

① Locate and double-click the entry you want to edit.

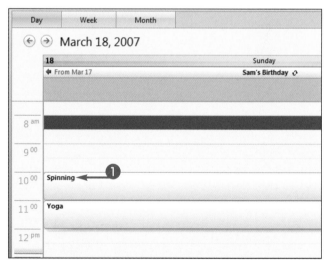

If the entry you want to open is part of a recurring series, Outlook asks whether you want to open only the entry you double-clicked or to open the entire series of recurring events.

② Click an entry option, the current entry in this example (◎ changes to ◉).

● Click here to open the entire series.

③ Click **OK**.

Note: If the entry you want to open is not part of a recurring series, skip Steps 2 and 3.

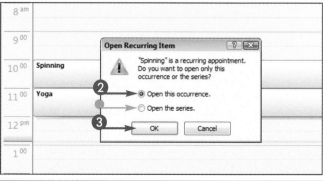

④ Make the necessary changes to the Calendar entry.

⑤ Click **Save & Close**.

● Outlook applies your changes.

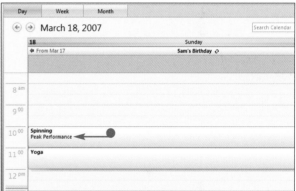

TIPS

Is there a quicker way to change a Calendar entry?

If an appointment, event, or meeting is moved to a different time, you can bypass opening the entry in its own window by simply clicking and dragging it to the desired time in Calendar. If its duration changes, click the edge of the entry in Calendar and drag to lengthen or shorten the entry. To edit the description of the entry, click and drag over the description to select it, and then type over the existing text with the new text.

How do I change a meeting?

Changing a meeting is a bit different from changing an appointment or event in that instead of clicking **Save & Close** to save your changes, you click **Send Update** to send the changes to the other meeting participants.

Create Additional Calendars

You can use Outlook to create and manage multiple calendars. For example, you might maintain one calendar for work and one for home. When you have additional calendars, you select the calendar you want to view from the navigation pane.

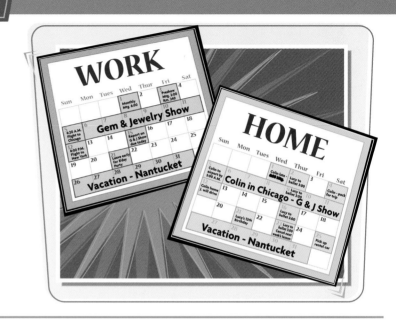

① With Calendar open, click **File**.

② Click **New**.

③ Click **Calendar**.

The Create New Folder dialog box appears, with the Calendar folder selected in the Select Where to Place the Folder list.

④ Type a name for the new calendar.

⑤ Click **OK**.

● Outlook adds the new calendar.

⑥ To view the new calendar, right-click it in the navigation pane.

⑦ Click **Open**.

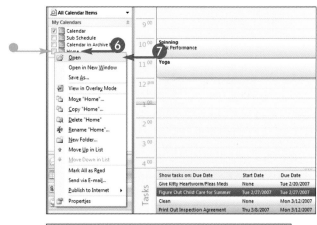

● Outlook switches the display to the new calendar.

TIPS

How do I add a Calendar entry to a different calendar?	**Can I open my new calendar in its own window?**
To add an appointment, event, or meeting to a calendar other than the one currently displayed, right-click the desired calendar in the navigation pane and click **Open** to switch to it. Then add the entry as normal. 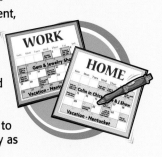	To open a different calendar in its own window, right-click the calendar in the navigation pane and choose **Open in New Window**. 

View Calendars in Overlay Mode

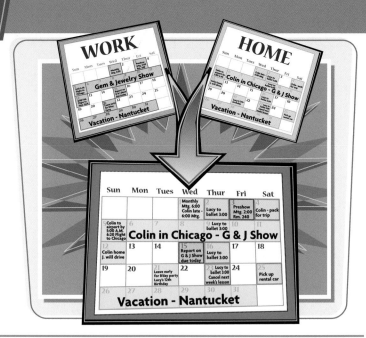

If you use Outlook to manage multiple calendars — for example, one for work and one for home — you can view those multiple calendars in overlay mode. In overlay mode, the calendars appear transparent and stacked, enabling you to see the appointments, events, and meetings in both.

View Calendars in Overlay Mode

1 With Calendar open, click the check box next to the calendar you want to view in addition to the one that is already open (☐ changes to ☑).

Note: You can view as many as 30 calendars at one time.

Outlook displays the selected calendars side by side.

2 To view the calendars in overlay mode, click the arrow (⬅) in the tab at the top of the calendar on the right.

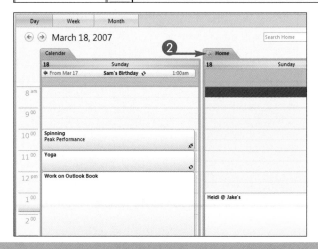

The calendars are displayed in overlay mode.

③ To revert to the original side-by-side view, click the arrow (→) in the tab of either calendar.

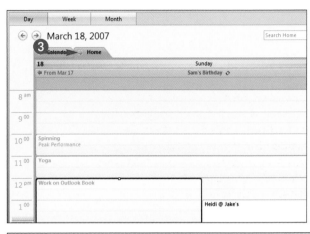

The calendars are again displayed side by side.

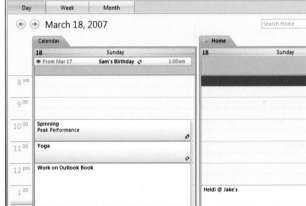

Can I copy Calendar entries from one calendar to another?

When calendars are in side-by-side mode, you can copy entries from one to the other. Simply click and drag the entry from one calendar to the other, releasing the mouse button when the entry is situated at the correct date and time.

Can I view three or more calendars in side-by-side and overlay mode?

Yes. To view two calendars in overlay, with a third calendar alongside it, open the two calendars you want stacked and follow the steps in this task to stack them. Then open the third calendar. When you do, it appears next to the two stacked calendars.

Create a Group Schedule

You can create group schedules to view the schedules of several people at once if you use Microsoft Exchange. For example, you might create a group schedule for the members of your team at work. That way, you can see your teammates' schedules at a glance. If you want, you can even send meeting invitations directly from the group schedule.

1 With Calendar open, click **Actions**.

2 Click **View Group Schedules**.

The Group Schedules dialog box appears.

3 Click **New**.

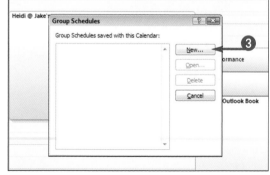

The Create New Group Schedule dialog box appears.

④ Type a name for the new group.

⑤ Click **OK**.

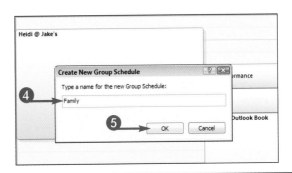

A new group schedule window opens, with the name you typed in the title bar.

⑥ Click the first field in the **Group Members** column.

⑦ Type the name of the first member of the group and press Enter.

● Alternatively, click **Add Others** and choose **Add from Address Book** or **Add from Public Folder** to select the necessary contacts.

Outlook retrieves contact information relating to the name you typed and displays the contact's schedule.

⑧ Repeat Step **7** to add more names to the list.

⑨ After you add the necessary names, click **Save and Close**.

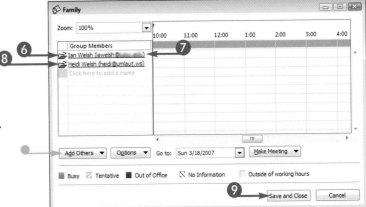

How do I view a group schedule I created?

To open the group schedule, click **Actions**, click **View Group Schedules**, and, in the Group Schedules dialog box that appears, click the group schedule you want to view and click **Open**.

How do I send a meeting request from the group schedule window?

To launch a meeting request or e-mail message either to the entire group or to certain members of the group, click **Make Meeting** and select the desired option from the list that appears.

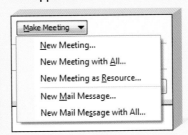

Send a Calendar Snapshot

You can e-mail a calendar snapshot to others — that is, a static view of your calendar as it appears at the moment it is sent. If the recipients of your calendar snapshot also use Outlook 2007, they can click and drag items from your calendar into theirs.

Send a Calendar Snapshot

① With Calendar open, click **Send a Calendar via E-mail**.

The Send a Calendar Via E-mail dialog box appears.

② Choose the calendar you want to send.

③ Select the date range you want to include in the snapshot.

④ Specify the calendar snapshot's level of detail.

⑤ Click **OK**.

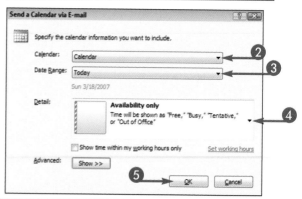

Outlook launches a new message window.

● The subject line is filled in automatically.

● The calendar snapshot is added as an attachment.

● Additionally, the calendar snapshot is embedded in the body of your message.

6 Type the necessary recipient information.

7 Add any additional text you want to include with the snapshot.

8 Click **Send**.

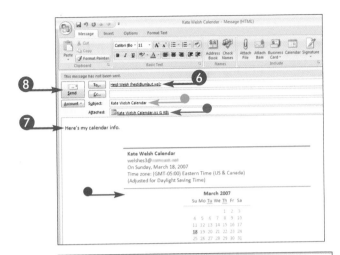

9 To verify that the message was sent, click **Mail**.

10 Click **Sent Items** in the folder list.

● The message appears in the Sent Items list.

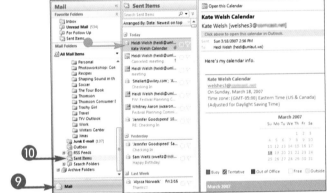

TIPS

Are there more snapshot options?
For more calendar snapshot options, click the **Show** button in the Send a Calendar via E-mail dialog box. Doing so reveals additional settings, including one that enables you to include details of the calendar marked private, to include attachments, and whether the layout of the calendar snapshot should be in Daily Schedule or List of Events form.

Can I change my working hours?
If you selected the **Show Time within My Working Hours Only** check box (☐ changes to ☑), you might want to define your working hours. To do so, click the **Set Working Hours** link in the Send a Calendar Via E-mail dialog box. Then, in the Calendar Options dialog box that appears, adjust the settings in the Calendar Work Week section (●) and click **OK**.

View a Calendar Snapshot

If someone mails you a calendar snapshot, you can view it on your own computer, and even drag items from the snapshot into your own calendar. Note that the calendar snapshot is static; it is not updated in your Outlook when changes are made to it by the person who sent it to you in his or her Outlook.

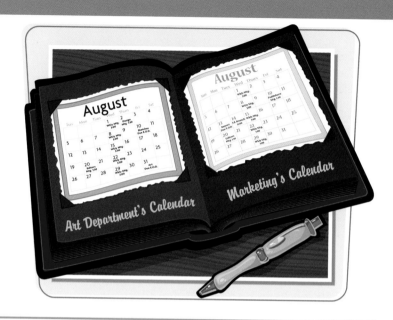

View a Calendar Snapshot

① In Mail, click the message in the message list that contains the calendar snapshot.

The message containing the calendar snapshot appears in the reading pane.

② Click **Open this Calendar**.

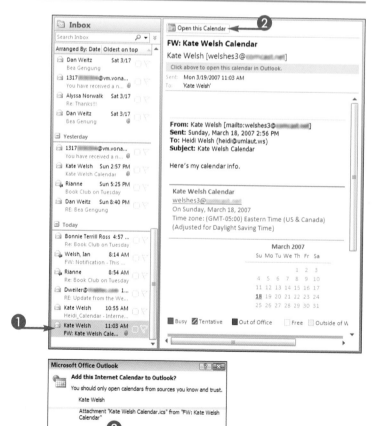

You are prompted to confirm that you want to add the calendar snapshot to Outlook.

③ Click **Yes**.

● Outlook adds the calendar snapshot, situating it side by side with whatever calendar is already displayed.

④ To copy an entry from the calendar snapshot to the other calendar that is displayed, click the entry in the snapshot to select it.

⑤ Click and drag the selected entry to the other calendar. When the appointment is over the desired time slot, release the mouse button.

● The appointment is copied from the calendar snapshot to the other calendar.

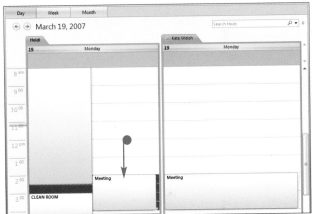

TIPS

How do I delete a calendar snapshot?

If you no longer need access to a calendar snapshot — or to any of your other calendars — you can delete it. To do so, right-click the calendar and choose **Delete Calendar Name** from the menu that appears.

How can I keep track of multiple calendars and snapshots?

If you are managing several calendars, you may find it difficult to locate the one you need. To mitigate this, Outlook enables you to group your calendars. For example, you might group all your family members' calendars together. To do so, click the **Add New Group** link in the navigation pane, type a name for the group, and click and drag any calendars you want to include in the group onto the group name.

Publish a Calendar on Office Online

You can *publish* a calendar on the Internet to share it with others. One way is to publish it on the Office Online Web site. The first time you publish a calendar on Office Online, you are prompted to register with the site.

Publish a Calendar on Office Online

① With Calendar open, in the navigation pane, right-click the calendar you want to publish.

② Click **Publish to Internet**.

③ Click **Publish to Office Online**.

● If this is the first time you have published a calendar to Office Online, you must register with the site using your Windows Live ID.

④ Click **Sign In**.

Note: *If you do not have a Windows Live account, click the **Sign Up for a Free Account** link and follow the on-screen instructions to create one.*

⑤ Type the e-mail address you used to register for your Windows Live account.

⑥ Type the password you set for the account.

⑦ Click **Sign In**.

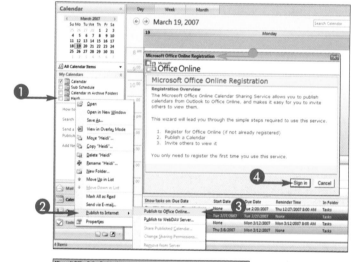

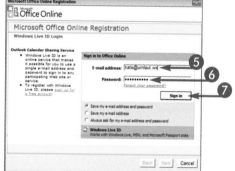

8 Click the **Service Agreement** link to read Microsoft's service agreement.

9 Click the **Microsoft Office Online Privacy Statement** link to read Microsoft's Office Online privacy policies.

10 Type your e-mail address.

11 Click **I Accept**.

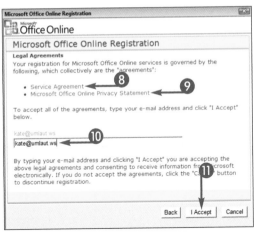

12 Type a display name, which is the name that will identify you on Office Online.

13 If necessary, choose your location from the **Country/Region** drop-down list.

14 To receive information about Microsoft products, security, and events, click this check box (changes to).

15 To receive information about products, security, and events from Microsoft partners, click this check box (changes to).

16 Click **Next**.

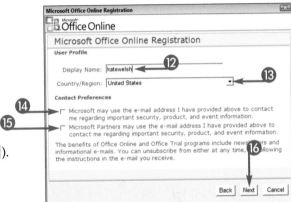

 TIPS

Can I share my published calendar with more people?

To share your calendar with more people after it is published, right-click the calendar in the navigation pane, choose **Publish to Internet**, and choose **Share Published Calendar**; in the new message window that appears, type the recipient and any additional body text, and click **Send**.

How do I revoke access from a published calendar?

To revoke access to a calendar published on Office Online, right-click the calendar, choose **Publish to Internet**, and choose **Change Sharing Permissions**. In the Remove Sharing Permissions dialog box, click the entry for the person whose privileges you want to revoke and click **Remove**.

continued

When you publish a calendar on Office Online, you set various sharing options, including whether the entire calendar should be shared or just a portion of it; the level of detail that should appear; whether changes you make in your Outlook calendar should be reflected in the published version; and so on.

Publish a Calendar on Office Online *(continued)*

⑰ Click **Finish**.

● In the Publish Calendar to Microsoft Office Online dialog box, select **Previous** and select a time range to publish only a portion of the calendar.

● Select **Whole Calendar** to publish the calendar in its entirety.

● Click here and select whether you want the published calendar to include full details, limited details, or availability information only.

● Click here to allow only invited users to view the calendar.

● Click here to allow anyone to view the calendar.

● If you opt to allow anyone to view the calendar, type some descriptive words about the calendar here. When other Office Online users search for terms you type, your calendar appears in the list of results.

⑱ Click **OK**.

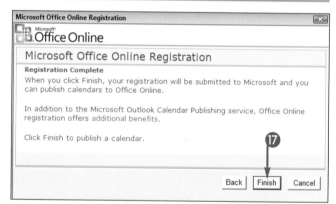

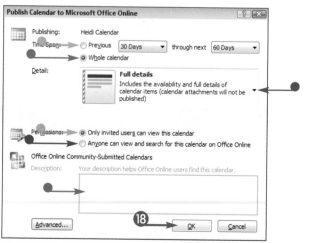

Outlook publishes the calendar and notifies you when the publishing operation is complete.

- To invite others to access your calendar, click **Yes**.

- If you do not want to invite anyone to access the calendar, click **No**.

  If you opted to invite others to access your calendar, Outlook launches a new message window.

- The subject line is filled in automatically.

⑲ Type the necessary recipient information.

⑳ Add any additional text you want to include with the snapshot.

㉑ Click **Send**.

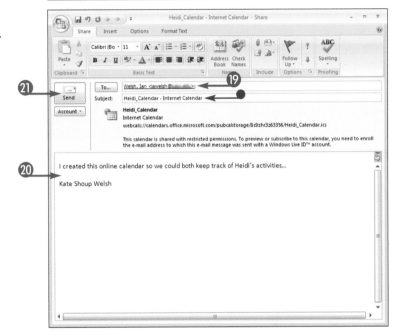

TIPS

What advanced options are available?
Clicking the **Advanced** button in the Publish Calendar to Microsoft Office Online dialog box launches the Published Calendar Settings dialog box. There, you can specify whether changes to your Outlook calendar should be uploaded to the published version automatically, and if so, whether the frequency with which these updates occur at the recommended interval.

How do I remove a calendar from Office Online?
If you no longer want to share a calendar with anyone, you can remove it from the server on which it is published. To do so, right-click the calendar in the navigation pane, choose **Publish to Internet**, and then **Remove from Server**.

If someone else invites you to access a calendar on Office Online, you can easily do so. Outlook gives you the option of simply previewing the calendar in your Web browser or subscribing to the calendar, meaning that when the original version of the calendar is updated, those updates are reflected in your version as well.

View and Subscribe to a Calendar on Office Online

PREVIEW A CALENDAR

1 In Mail, click the message in the message list that contains the invitation to view the calendar on Office Online.

The message containing the invitation appears in the reading pane.

2 Click **Preview this Calendar**.

● You are prompted to confirm that you want to view the calendar in your Web browser.

3 Click **Yes**.

Note: *You are prompted to log in to Windows Live; supply the e-mail address and password you supplied when you created your account. If you do not have a Windows Live account, click the **Sign Up for a Free Account** link and follow the on-screen instructions to create one.*

The calendar is displayed in your Web browser.

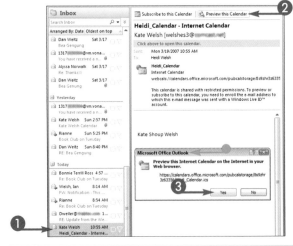

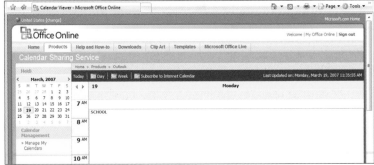

SUBSCRIBE TO A CALENDAR

1 In Mail, click the message in the message list that contains the invitation to view the calendar on Office Online.

The message containing the invitation appears in the reading pane.

2 Click **Subscribe to this Calendar**.

● You are prompted to confirm that you want to add the calendar to Outlook and subscribe to updates.

3 Click **Yes**.

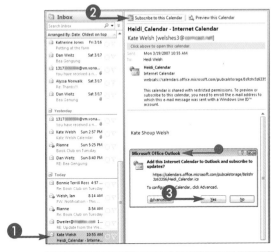

● Outlook adds the calendar, situating it side by side with whatever calendar is already displayed.

TIPS

Can I make changes to an Office Online calendar to which I subscribe?

You can view the contents of a calendar to which you subscribe, including updates made to the original calendar by the person who manages it. You cannot, however, make changes to the calendar.

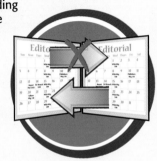

Can I copy entries in a subscription calendar to my own calendar?

To copy an entry from the subscription calendar to the other calendar that is displayed, click the entry in the subscription calendar to select it, and click and drag the selected entry to the other calendar. When the entry is over the desired time slot, release the mouse button. The entry is copied from the subscription calendar to the other calendar.

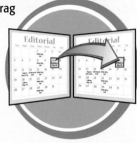

Subscribe to an Internet Calendar

In addition to subscribing to calendars on Office Online, you can also subscribe to other Internet calendars, called *iCalendars.* For example, you might subscribe to an iCalendar that contains the schedule for your favorite team. (To see what types of iCalendars are available that might interest you, visit a site such as iCalShare.com.)

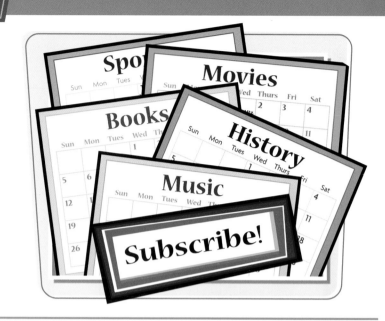

Subscribe to an Internet Calendar

① Click **Start**.

The Windows Start menu opens.

② Locate and click the menu entry for your Web browser.

Windows launches your Web browser.

③ After locating an iCalendar to which you want to subscribe (here, a World Cup cricket schedule on iCalShare.com), click the **Subscribe** (or similarly named) link.

You are prompted to confirm that you want to add the iCalendar to Outlook and subscribe to updates.

4️⃣ Click **Yes**.

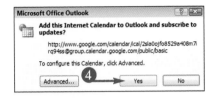

● Outlook adds the iCalendar, situating it side by side with whatever calendar is already displayed.

TIPS

Can I make changes to an iCalendar to which I subscribe?

You can view the contents of an iCalendar to which you subscribe, including updates made to the original calendar by the person who manages it. You cannot, however, make changes to the calendar.

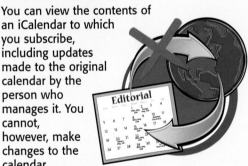

What is the best way to manage my iCalendars?

Outlook enables you to add, change, or remove iCalendars from one easy location: the Account Settings dialog box. To access these iCalendar settings, click the **Tools** menu and then **Account Settings**, and, in the Account Settings dialog box, click the **Internet Calendars** tab (●).

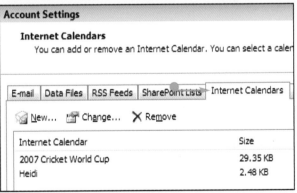

Save a Calendar as a Web Page

If you manage your own Web site — for example, for your child's Little League team — you can save your Outlook calendar as a Web page and post it. Others can then visit your site to view the calendar. (When you save a calendar as a Web page, it is not updated to reflect changes made to the calendar on your computer.)

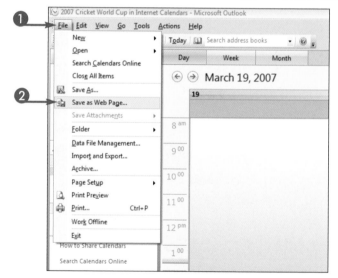

Save a Calendar as a Web Page

1. With the calendar you want to save as a Web page displayed in Outlook, click **File**.

2. Click **Save As Web Page**.

3. In the Save as Web Page dialog box, click ▾ and select the first and last dates you want to include in the Web page.

4. To allow page visitors to view details about the appointments in the calendar, select the **Include Appointment Details** check box.

● To include a background graphic for the Web page, select the **Use Background Graphic** check box and click **Browse** to locate the graphic.

5. Type a calendar name.

6. To open the Web page in your Web browser after you finish the save operation, select the **Open Saved Web Page in Browser** check box.

7. To locate the folder in which you want to save the Web page file, click **Browse**.

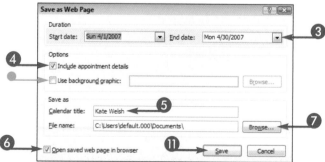

The Calendar File Name dialog box appears.

⑧ Locate and open the folder in which you want to save the Web page file.

⑨ Type a descriptive name for the file.

⑩ Click **Select** in the Calendar File Name dialog box.

⑪ Click **Save** in the Save as Web Page dialog box.

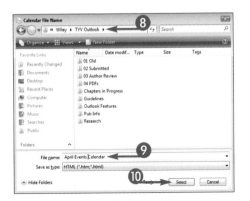

Windows launches your Web browser with the calendar displayed in Web page form.

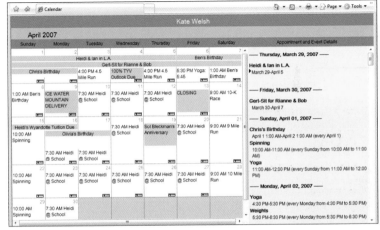

TIPS

How do I post my calendar on my site?

The details of posting your calendar to your site depend on what type of software you use to design the site. For more information, refer to the site-building software's help files.

How do I publish my calendar to a WebDAV server?

Assuming your ISP supports it, you can publish your calendar to a WebDAV server, which enables users to collaboratively edit and manage files. To do so, right-click the calendar you want to publish, click **Publish to Internet**, and then **Publish to WebDAV Server**. In the dialog box that appears, specify the Web server's URL and the folder in which your calendar should be stored; the dates that should be visible in the shared calendar; and the level of detail that should appear.

Print a
Calendar

If you know you will be away
from your computer but will
need access to your schedule,
you can print it. Depending on
which view of the calendar is
displayed, you can print your
daily schedule, weekly schedule,
or monthly schedule.

Print a Calendar

1 Switch to the view you want to print
(here, Month).

2 Click **File**.

3 Click **Print Preview**.

The Print Preview window opens,
showing how the calendar printout
will look.

4 Click **Print**.

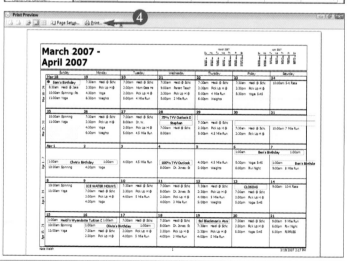

The Print dialog box appears.

● If necessary, click the **Name** ▾ and select a different printer.

● You can select a different calendar here.

● If you want, you can switch to a different view style, such as Daily Style or Weekly Style.

● Use the Print Range settings to change the range of dates printed.

● Optionally, click the **Hide Details of Private Appointments** check box to omit them from the printout (☐ changes to ☑).

● Click here to change the number of pages printed.

● Type the number of copies you want to print.

● To collate multiple copies, click the **Collate Copies** check box (☐ changes to ☑).

5 Click **OK**.

Outlook sends the calendar to the printer.

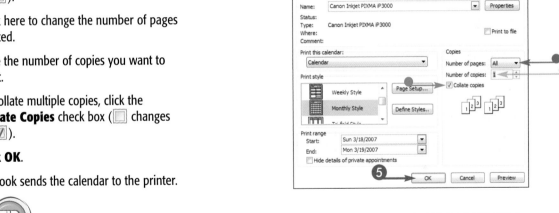

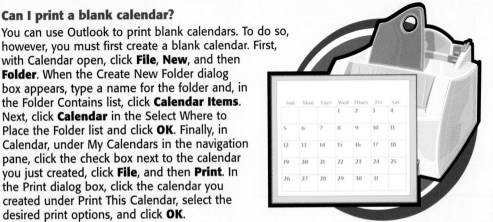

TIP

Can I print a blank calendar?

You can use Outlook to print blank calendars. To do so, however, you must first create a blank calendar. First, with Calendar open, click **File**, **New**, and then **Folder**. When the Create New Folder dialog box appears, type a name for the folder and, in the Folder Contains list, click **Calendar Items**. Next, click **Calendar** in the Select Where to Place the Folder list and click **OK**. Finally, in Calendar, under My Calendars in the navigation pane, click the check box next to the calendar you just created, click **File**, and then **Print**. In the Print dialog box, click the calendar you created under Print This Calendar, select the desired print options, and click **OK**.

Using Outlook's Task Component

Outlook's Task component enables you to keep track of the things you need to do. You might use Outlook's Tasks feature to manage a daily list of activities or to keep track of steps you need to complete in order to finish a project.

You can create entries for your To-Do list, displayed in Outlook's Tasks window, in much the same way as you create entries for your Outlook calendar. An entry represents a task you need to complete. After you create an entry, it is added to your To-Do list.

Create a New Task

① If Contacts is not currently open, click the **Tasks** button in the navigation pane.

Outlook switches to Task mode.

② Click the **New** button.

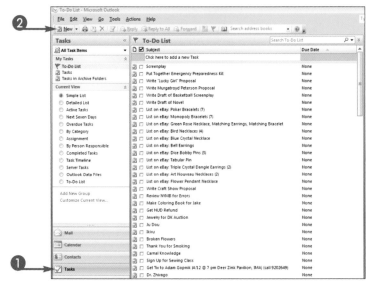

Outlook displays a new task window.

③ In the Subject field, type a description of your task.

④ Type a due date for the task.

⑤ Click the **Status** ▾ and click a progress option.

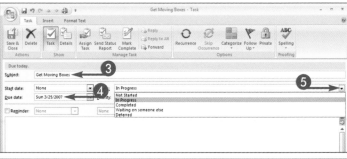

6 Type a note or details about the task here.

● Optionally, click the **Priority** ▼ and choose a priority level for the task.

● Optionally, click the **% Complete** ▲ to specify how much of the task is finished.

7 Click **Save & Close**.

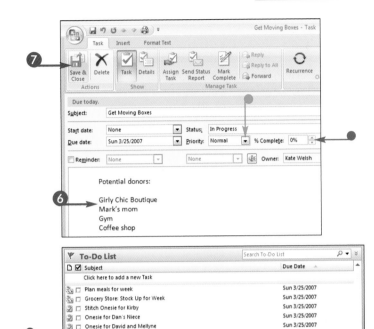

● Outlook displays the task in the To-Do list.

What if my task is recurring?

If your task is recurring, such as paying the mortgage or taking out the trash, you can specify that in Outlook; Outlook regenerates the task using the parameters you set. To do so, click the **Recurrence** button in the new task window and, in the Task Recurrence dialog box that appears, specify whether the task recurs daily, weekly, monthly, or yearly; indicate when the recurrence pattern should end; and set other recurrence parameters.

Is there a quicker way to add a task?

You can bypass the new task window and instead enter a task directly into the Tasks window. To do so, click **Click Here to Add a Task** at the top of the task list, type a description for your new task, and press Enter.

Attach a File to a Task Entry

Outlook makes it easy to attach files to Task entries. Suppose, for example, that you have created a Task entry to review a document for a colleague. You might attach the document that needs to be reviewed to the task entry for quick retrieval.

① Create a task.

② Click the **Insert** tab in the new task window.

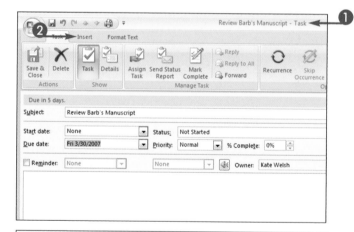

Outlook displays the Ribbon's Insert tab.

③ Click **Attach File**.

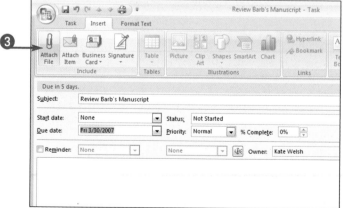

The Insert File dialog box appears.

④ Locate and click the file you want to attach to the task.

⑤ Click **Insert**.

● The file is attached to the task.

⑥ Click the **Close** button (☒) to close the task.

⑦ When prompted, click **Yes** to save changes to the task.

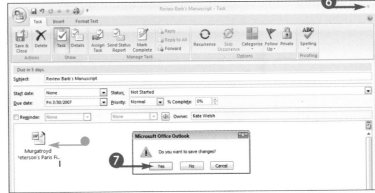

 TIPS

How do I open the attached file?

To open a file attached to a task, simply double-click the icon representing the file in the task window.

Can I attach an Outlook item to a task?

In addition to attaching a file such as a Word document or image file to a task entry, you can also attach Outlook items, such as e-mail messages, Contact entries, and Calendar entries. To do so, click **Attach Item** (●) in the task entry's Insert tab; the Insert Item dialog box appears. Click the folder that contains the type of Outlook item you want to attach, locate and click the desired item, and click **OK**.

By default, tasks are displayed by
due date, with limited information
about each task appearing in the
To-Do list. Outlook enables you to
sort and view your tasks in myriad
other ways, however. For example,
you might view only those tasks
due in the next seven days. In
addition, you can create custom
sort parameters.

Sort Tasks

PERFORM A SIMPLE SORT

1 In the navigation pane, click the criterion
by which you want to sort or view your
messages (◉ changes to ◉).

In this example, **Next Seven Days** is
selected.

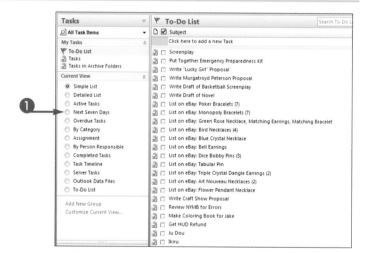

Outlook sorts the messages by the view
or sort criterion you select.

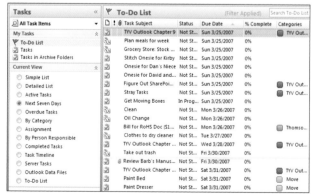

PERFORM A CUSTOM SORT

① Click **View**.

② Click **Arrange By**.

③ Click **Custom**.

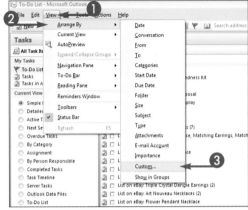

④ In the Customize View dialog box, click **Sort**.

⑤ In the Sort dialog box, click the **Sort Items By** ☐ and choose the parameter by which you want to sort (here, **Due Date**).

⑥ If you want the tasks to appear with those that are due soonest displayed first, select the **Ascending** option; to display them from last to first, select the **Descending** option.

⑦ Repeat Steps **5** and **6** in as many Then By fields as necessary to enter the rest of your sort parameters.

⑧ Click **OK** to close the Sort dialog box.

⑨ Click **OK** to close the Customize View dialog box.

Your tasks are sorted accordingly.

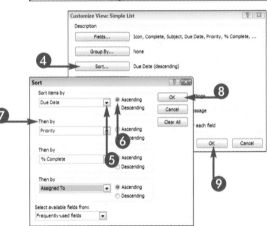

TIP

How does grouping work?

You can group your tasks by criteria. For example, if your tasks have been sorted by due date, you can group them so that all tasks due on a particular date, week, or month are grouped (depending on how soon the task's due date is). To group tasks, click **View**, **Arrange By**, and then **Show in Groups**. You can collapse a group (that is, hide all the tasks within the group, showing only the group header) or expand a group (revealing the tasks that were hidden when the group was collapsed) by clicking ☐ or ☐, respectively (●).

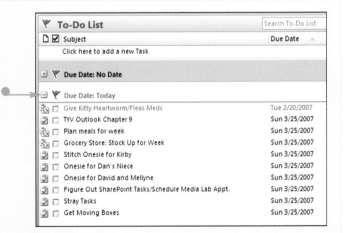

View a Task Entry and Explore Editing Options

When you open a task entry, you see information particulars you entered when the task was added, as well as any subsequent changes. You edit a task in much the same way you create a task: by typing information in the fields in the task window and choosing options from the task window's Ribbon.

View a Task Entry and Explore Editing Options

① Double-click the task you want to open.

Outlook opens the task in its own window, with the Task tab displayed.

● View or edit details about the task, such as its description, start date, end date, status, priority, and/or percentage complete.

● Icons representing files attached to the task appear here.

● View or edit notes about the task.

② Click the **Insert** tab.

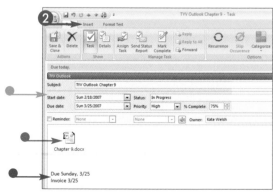

Outlook displays the Insert tab.

● Click any of these options to add items to the note area, such as files, tables, illustrations, links, text-related objects, or symbols.

③ Click the **Format Text** tab.

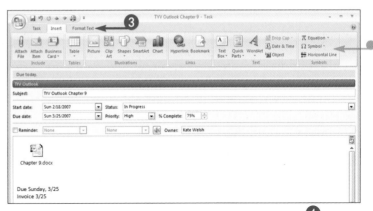

Outlook displays the Format Text tab.

● Click any of these options to format text in the note area.

④ Click the **Close** button (⊠) to close the task.

⑤ When prompted, click **Yes** to save changes to the task.

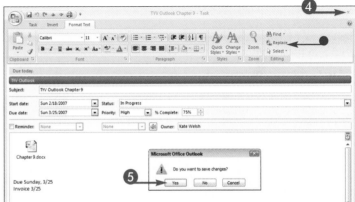

What if I cannot find the task I want to open?

You can use Outlook's Instant Search feature to quickly locate the task you want to open. To do so, type a keyword you know appears in the task entry in the Search field found in the upper-right corner of the Tasks window; Outlook locates and displays all entries that contain the keyword you typed. When you locate the entry you seek in the list of matching entries, double-click it to open it in its own window.

What happens if I click the Details button?

Click the **Details** button (●) in the Task tab to view and type additional details about the task, such as the date the task is slated to be completed, how much time has been spent on the task, and more.

Link a Task to a Contact

Suppose, for example, that you offer to help someone write a report; in addition to creating a task entry for your To-Do list to remember to help with the report, you might also link the task to the contact entry for the person who needs your help. That way, when you open the task, your contact's information is easily accessible.

LINK A TASK TO A CONTACT

1 Create or open the task you want to link to a contact entry.

2 Click **Contacts**.

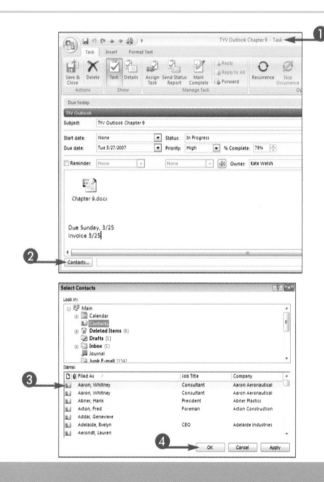

The Select Contacts dialog box appears.

3 Click the contact you want to link to this task entry to select it.

4 Click **OK**.

● A link to the contact entry is added to the task.

5 Click **Save & Close** to close the task window.

OPEN A LINKED CONTACT

1 To open a linked contact from within a task, first open the task window.

2 Click the contact link.

● Outlook opens the contact in its own window.

3 To view the task from within the contact, click **Activities**.

● The task appears in the Activities window.

What if the Contacts button is missing?

If there is no Contacts button in the task window, follow these steps. Click **Tools** and then **Options**. The Options dialog box appears with the Preferences tab displayed. Click **Contact Options**. The Contact Options dialog box appears. Click the **Show Contact Linking on All Forms** check box (□ changes to ☑).

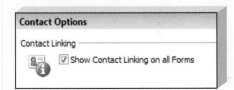

Can I integrate a task into Calendar?

Tasks are automatically visible from Calendar, but only in Day or Week view. You can even enter new tasks from within Calendar by clicking the empty space at the bottom of the task list. To remove the task list from view in Calendar, or to change how it is displayed, click **View**, **Daily Task List**, and select the desired option from the submenu that appears.

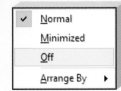

Delegate a Task

You can delegate a task to another person, who can accept or decline the assignment. When someone accepts a task, that person becomes the *owner* of the task; only the owner can make changes to the task. If a task is declined, the person who created the task can revert ownership back to himself.

See the next task for more information on accepting or declining tasks.

① Create or open the task you want to delegate.

② In the Task tab's Manage Tasks group, click **Assign Task**.

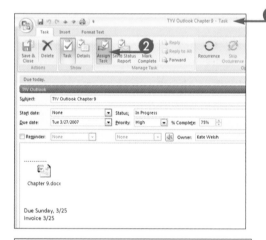

The task window changes to a message window.

③ Type the name or e-mail address of the person to whom you want to delegate the task.

● The name of the task becomes the subject of the e-mail message.

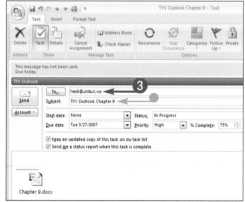

● The Start Date, Due Date, Status, Priority, and % Complete fields reflect the settings you established when you created the task.

④ To keep an updated copy of the task on your own task list, click this check box (☐ changes to ☑).

⑤ To receive a status report when the task is complete, click this check box (☐ changes to ☑).

⑥ Type a message to the task recipient.

⑦ Click Send.

⑧ To verify that the task assignment was sent, click **Mail** in the navigation pane.

⑨ Click the **Sent Items** folder in the navigation pane's folder list.

● The message containing the task appears in the message list.

Note: *To view tasks that you have delegated to other users, click* **View** *while in Task mode, click* **Current View***, and then* **Assignment***.*

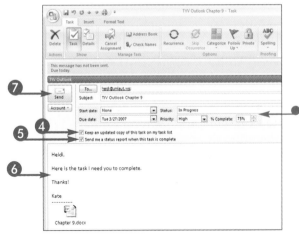

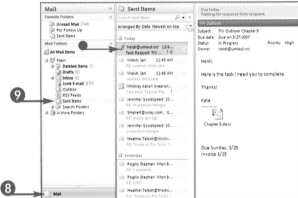

TIPS

How do I track the status of an assigned task?

When the person to whom you delegated a task updates the task, all copies of the task — including the version in your Outlook — are also updated automatically (assuming you checked the **Keep an Updated Copy of this Task on My Task List** check box). When the person marks the task complete, you are automatically sent a status report notifying you of the task's completion (assuming you checked the **Send Me a Status Report When this Task is Complete** check box).

Can I delegate tracking duties?

You can assign tracking duties to someone else. To do so, open the task you want someone else to track and, in the Manage Task group on the Task tab, click **Forward**. Type the e-mail information for the intended recipient, type your message, and click **Send**. The person to whom you forward the message receives the task's status reports.

Accept or Decline a Task Assignment

Just as you can delegate tasks to others, others can also delegate tasks to you. When you receive a message with an assigned task, you can accept the assignment or decline it.

ACCEPT A TASK ASSIGNMENT

1 Click **Mail** to switch to Outlook Mail.

2 Click the message in the message list that contains the task assignment.

Outlook displays the message in the reading pane.

3 Click **Accept**.

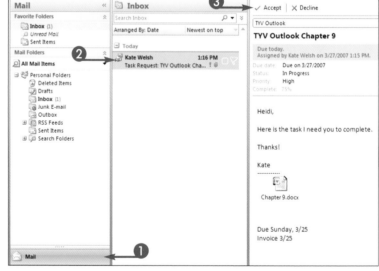

The Accepting Task dialog box appears.

4 Click the **Edit the Response Before Sending** option to edit your response before sending it (◎ changes to ◉).

● To send the response without editing it, click the **Send the Response Now** option (◎ changes to ◉).

5 Click **OK**.

214

If you opt to edit the response before sending it, Outlook opens a message window containing the task.

⑥ Edit the response as desired.

⑦ Click **Send**.

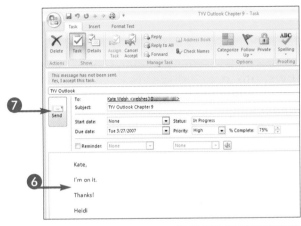

● The person who delegated the task to you receives an e-mail indicating that you accept the assignment.

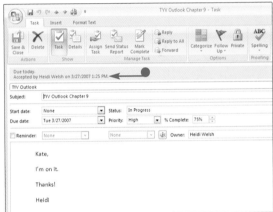

 TIPS

How do I decline an assignment?

To reject an assignment, simply click **Decline** rather than Accept in the message containing the task assignment. As when you accept a task, you have the option of sending the message declining the task immediately (●), or to edit it first.

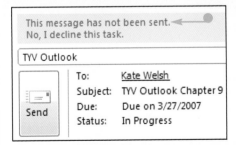

What happens if I decline an assignment?

Even if you decline an assignment, you remain its owner until the person who attempted to assign the task to you reclaims ownership of it. To reclaim ownership of a task, that person much locate and open the original message he or she sent containing the assignment request and click **Return to Task List** in the Task tab's Manage Task group.

Send a Status Report for a Task

You may need to update your manager or some other person as to the status of a task. This information can include whether the task is complete, in progress, or not started; how much of the task is complete; how many hours have been spent on the task; and so on.

① Double-click the task for which you want to send a status report.

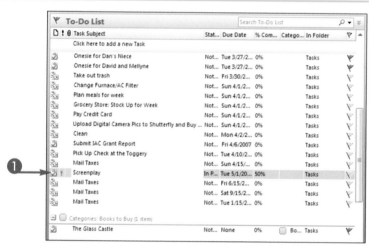

The task opens in its own window.

② Click **Send Status Report**.

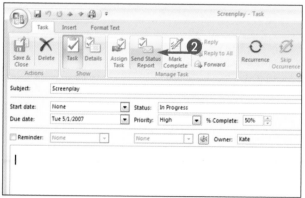

Outlook launches a message window with the status information included.

● The Subject field is already filled in.

● The status information appears here.

③ Type the recipient's e-mail address.

④ Type any message you want to accompany your report.

⑤ Click **Send**.

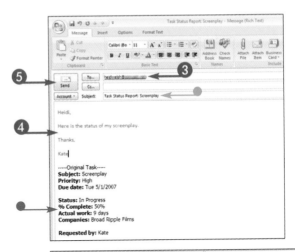

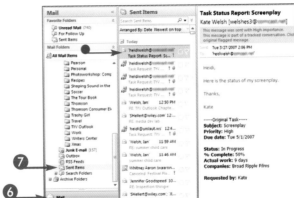

⑥ To confirm that the report was sent, click **Mail**.

⑦ Click **Sent Items**.

● The message containing the report appears in the message list.

 TIPS

How do I send a status report for an assigned task?

You send a status report for a task that has been assigned to you in much the same way as you send a status report for any other task. To do so, open the task in its own window and, on the Task tab, in the Manage Tasks group, click **Send Status Report**. The name of the person who assigned the task to you is added automatically to the To field (●), as are other names associated with the task.

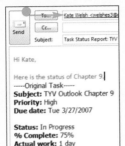

How do I send a comment about an assigned task?

In addition to sending a status report about a task, you can also send comments; to do so, click **Reply** or **Reply All** instead of Send Status Report in the task window. The resulting message window automatically includes the person who assigned the task to you; if you clicked **Reply All**, other names associated with the task also appear. Simply type your comment and click **Send**.

Mark a Task as Complete

When you finish with a task, you can mark it as complete. When a task is marked complete, it remains in your task list, but with a strikethrough-style font.

Mark a Task as Complete

① In Tasks mode, double-click the task you want to mark as complete.

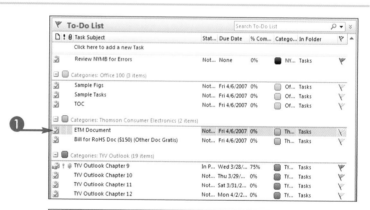

The task opens in its own window.

② In the Task tab's Manage Task group, click **Mark Complete**.

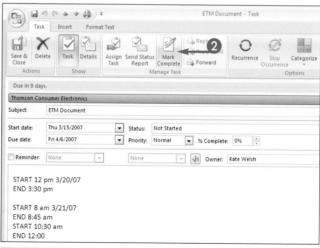

● The task remains in the task list, but with a strikethrough font, and with a check mark in the flag column.

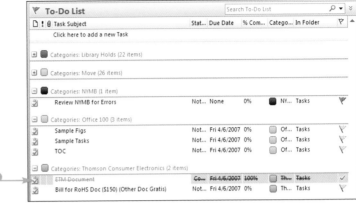

3 To permanently remove the task from the task list, you must delete it. To begin, right-click the task.

4 Click **Delete** from the menu that appears.

Outlook deletes the task.

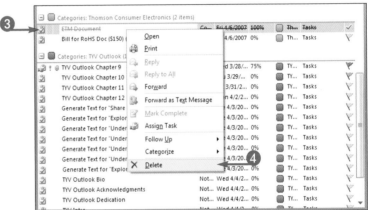

Can I hide completed tasks rather than deleting them?

To hide completed tasks, so that they are no longer displayed in your To-Do list, but retain them in Outlook, click **Active Tasks** (●) under Current View in the navigation pane.

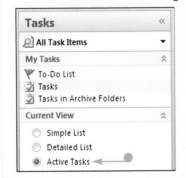

Can I color-code completed tasks?

To make it a bit easier to spot completed tasks, you can change their color. To do so, click **Tools**, and then **Options**. In the Options dialog box that appears, click **Task Options** in the Preferences tab. The Task Options dialog box appears; click the **Completed Task Color** ▣ and select the color you want to assign completed tasks (●). Note that you can also change the color of overdue tasks here.

Print Your Task List and Task Items

If you know you will be traveling to a location in which you will not have access to a computer, you can print a hard copy of your Outlook tasks either individually or in list form.

PRINT YOUR TASK LIST

① If you want to print only certain tasks, click them in the task list to select them. To print the entire list, skip to Step **2**.

② Click **File**.

③ Click **Print**.

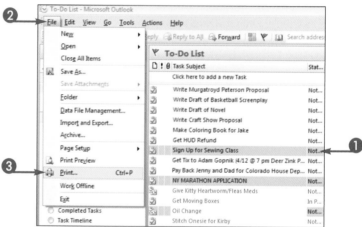

The Print dialog box appears.

④ Specify the desired print style – **Table Style** (as shown here) or **Memo Style**.

Note: *If you want your list to look similar to the list as it is presented in Outlook, choose **Table Style**.*

⑤ To print all of your tasks, select **All Rows**. To print only the entries you selected, select **Only Selected Rows**.

Note: *If you choose **Memo Style** instead of Table Style in Step **4**, you do not have the option of choosing All Rows or Selected Rows. You do, however, have the option of printing any files attached to your tasks.*

⑥ Click **OK** to print the list.

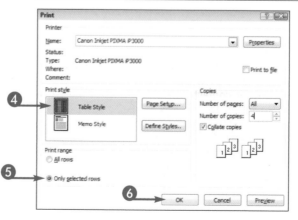

PRINT A SINGLE TASK ENTRY

1 Double-click the task you want to print to open it in its own window.

2 Click the **Print Preview** button (📄) in the contact window's Quick Access toolbar.

*Note: If you do not need to preview the task before you print it, simply click the **Print** button (🖨️) in the Quick Access toolbar. Note, however, that Outlook does not launch a Print dialog box if you click this button, meaning you cannot set print preferences.*

3 In the Print Preview window, review the task information.

4 Click the **Print** button.

● The Print dialog box appears.

Note: Single tasks can be printed only in Memo style.

5 To print any attachments associated with the contact, select **Print Attached Files**.

6 Click **OK** to print the task.

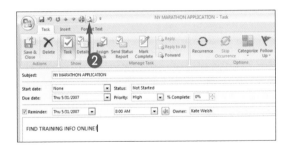

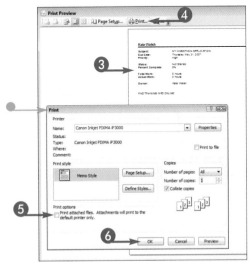

How do I select multiple tasks?

To select multiple contacts that are adjacent to each other in the list, hold down the Shift key on your keyboard as you first click the topmost contact you want to select, and then click the bottom-most contact you want to select. To select contacts that are scattered throughout the list, hold down the Ctrl key on your keyboard as you click each contact that you want to print.

Where is my Print Preview button?

If the Print Preview button (📄) is not visible in the contact window, click 🔽 in the top-left area of the window and choose **Print Preview**.

Using Notes
and Journal Entries

Sometimes, what you need to keep organized is not a task or calendar entry, but rather a simple note for further reference. To accommodate this, Outlook includes a Notes feature; it acts much like the omnipresent sticky note. Outlook also offers a Journal feature, for jotting down notes relating to phone calls, meetings, and so on.

Create
a Note

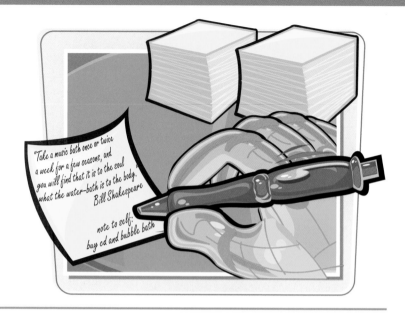

Being able to jot down a quick note is an essential component of keeping organized. To accommodate this, Outlook boasts a Notes feature that is similar to a sticky note in the physical world.

Create a Note

1 Click **File**.

2 Click **New**.

3 Click **Note**.

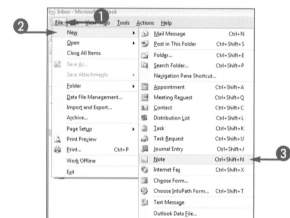

● Outlook opens a blank note.

4 Type the text you want to appear in the note.

5 Click the **Close** button (☒) to close the note.

Viewing your notes is as easy as creating them. Simply open the Notes folder and double-click the note you want to view. When you view a note, you see the note's text, as well as the date and time when the note was created.

View Notes

① Click the **Notes** button (🗒) at the bottom of the navigation pane.

Outlook switches to Notes mode.

② Double-click the note you want to view.

● Outlook opens the note.

Sort
Notes

If you create so many notes you cannot reasonably find the one you need, you can sort them. One way to sort your messages is to switch to Notes List view in order to view your notes in table form; you can then sort alphabetically by subject, by date created, by category, and so on.

① If necessary, click the **Notes** button (▦) at the bottom of the navigation pane to switch to Notes view.

② Click **Notes List** (◉ changes to ◉) in the navigation pane.

Outlook switches to Notes List view.

③ To sort notes, click the desired column header.

Note: In this example, the Subject column header is clicked to sort the notes alphabetically.

Note: You can also opt to view only those notes created during the last seven days or to sort notes by category. (You learn how to categorize Outlook items in Chapter 11.)

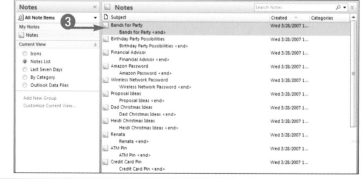

The notes are sorted (here, alphabetically by subject).

④ Locate and double-click the note you want to view.

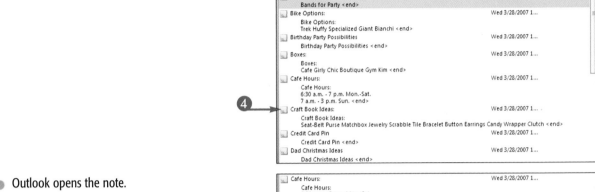

● Outlook opens the note.

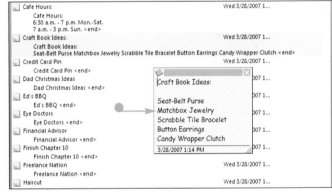

TIPS

Can I perform a custom sort?

Yes. To do so, click the **Customize Current View** link in the navigation pane and, in the Customize View dialog box that appears, click **Sort**. Select the desired sort parameters and click **OK**.

Can I change how note icons are displayed?

If you are in Icons view, as opposed to Notes List view, you can click **Large Icons**, **Small Icons**, or **List** (●) to change how the note icons are displayed.

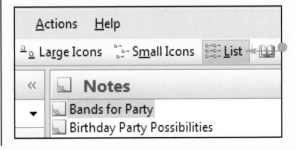

Print
Notes

You can print your Outlook notes. In addition to printing individual notes, you can print a list of all your notes, provided the notes are displayed in Notes List view. You might print a note to pass it on to someone else.

Print Notes

PRINT A SINGLE NOTE

1 If necessary, click the **Notes** button (□) at the bottom of the navigation pane to switch to Notes view.

2 Double-click the note you want to print.

● The note opens.

3 Click the **Notes** menu button (▣).

4 Click **Print**.

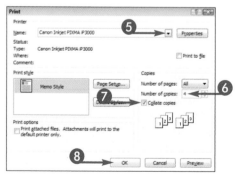

The Print dialog box appears.

5 Select the printer you want to use.

6 Type the number of copies of the note you want to print.

7 If you are printing multiple copies and you want them to be collated, click the **Collate Copies** check box (▣ changes to ▣).

8 Click **OK**.

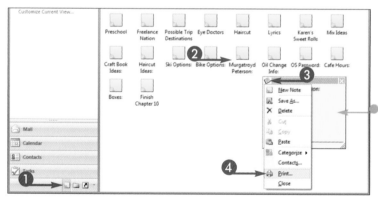

PRINT A LIST OF NOTES

① To print only certain notes, select them. To print the entire list, skip to Step **2**.

② Click **File**.

③ Click **Print**.

The Print dialog box appears.

④ Choose a printer.

⑤ Choose a print style – **Table Style** or **Memo Style**.

Note: *Choose Table Style to print a list that looks similar to the list in Outlook.*

⑥ To print all of your notes, select **All Rows**. To print only the notes you selected, select **Only Selected Rows**.

Note: *If you chose Memo Style in Step 5, the All Rows and Selected Rows options are not available. Instead, you can specify that any files attached to the notes be printed.*

⑦ Type the number of copies you want to print.

⑧ If you are printing multiple copies, and you want them to be collated, select the **Collate Copies** check box.

⑨ Click **OK**.

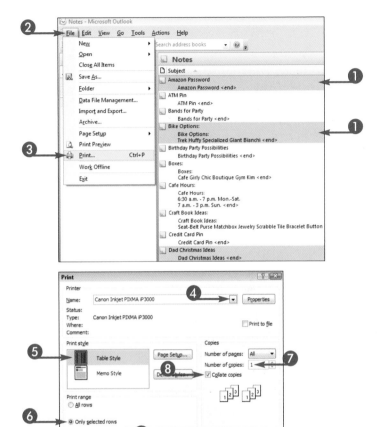

TIPS

Is there a quicker way to print a note?

If you know you do not need to set printer options, you can bypass the Print dialog box, sending your note straight to the printer. To do so, right-click the note icon or entry in Notes view and choose **Print** from the menu that appears.

Are there other ways to share notes?

In addition to printing notes, you can share notes by e-mailing them to others. To do so, right-click the icon or list entry for note you want to send and choose **Forward** from the menu that appears; Outlook launches a new message window with the note added as an attachment.

Record Journal Entries Automatically

To keep track of your interactions with contacts and other activities, such as the amount of time spent on a particular project, you can use Outlook's Journal feature. Perhaps the most efficient way to use this feature is to configure it to log certain activities automatically.

Record Journal Entries Automatically

① Click **Tools**.

② Click **Options**.

The Options dialog box appears, with the Preferences tab displayed.

③ Click **Journal Options**.

The Journal Options dialog box appears.

④ Under Automatically Record These Items, select the check boxes next to the items for which you want to generate automatic journal entries.

⑤ Under For These Contacts, select the check box next to each contact for which items should be automatically recorded.

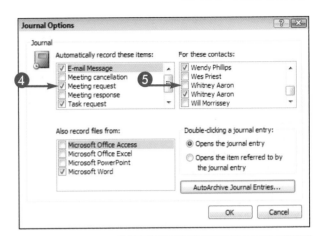

⑥ Optionally, in addition to recording activities related to Outlook, you can record activities related to other Office programs. To do so, select the necessary check boxes under Also Record Files From.

⑦ Specify whether double-clicking a journal entry opens the entry or opens the item to which the entry refers.

⑧ Click **OK**.

⑨ Click OK to close the Options dialog box.

Outlook records journal entries automatically.

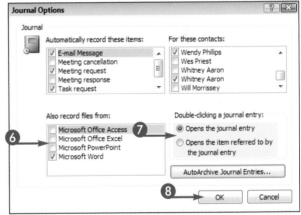

TIPS

What happens if I click the AutoArchive Journal Entries button?

Failing to archive journal entries — especially if they are generated automatically — can quickly result in overconsumption of hard drive space on your computer. To ensure that your journal entries do not consume more than their fair share, Outlook archives them automatically using default archive settings. Clicking **AutoArchive Journal Entries** in the Journal Options dialog box opens the Journal Properties dialog box, where you can change these AutoArchive settings.

How do I stop automatically recording journal entries?

To disable automatic journal entries, open the Journal Options dialog box and deselect the check boxes under Automatically Record These Items and Also Record Files From.

Add a Journal Entry Manually

In addition to configuring Outlook to log journal entries automatically (discussed in the previous task), you can add them manually. These journal entries can relate to Outlook items or activities relating to other files on your computer.

RECORD AN OUTLOOK ITEM

1 Click **File**.

2 Click **New**.

3 Click **Journal Entry**.

4 In the new journal entry window, type a subject for the journal entry.

5 Click the **Entry Type** and choose what type of activity you want to log.

6 Type the name of the company to which the activity relates.

7 Click **Start Time** and choose the date and time at which the activity you want to record occurred.

8 Click the **Duration** and specify how much time was spent on the activity.

9 Type any notes about the activity.

10 Click **Save & Close**.

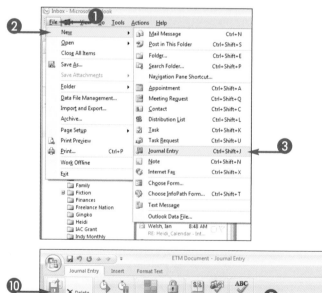

RECORD OTHER ACTIVITIES

① Click **Go**.

② Click **Journal**, and Outlook switches to Journal mode.

③ Open the folder on your hard drive that contains the file for which you want to record your activities, click the file, and then drag the file from its window to the Journal window.

● The subject line of the new entry window for the file contains the name of the file.

● The Entry Type field contains the type of file you selected.

● The Start Time drop-down lists contain today's date and the current time.

● An icon representing the file appears here; you can double-click it to open the file.

④ Type the name of the company to which the activity relates.

⑤ Type any notes about the activity.

⑥ Click **Save & Close**.

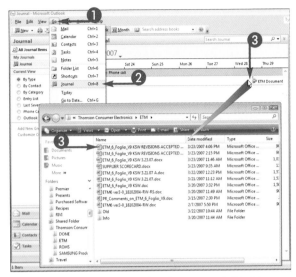

TIPS

How does the Timer feature work?
You can use Journal's Timer feature to keep track of time spent on an activity such as a phone call or meeting. To use the feature, create or open the journal entry for the activity and click the **Start Timer** button in the journal window. To pause the timer, click **Pause Timer**.

Can I associate a journal entry with a contact?
To associate a journal entry with a particular contact, click the **Contacts** button in the bottom-left corner of the journal entry window and choose the contact from the Select Contacts dialog box that appears. If no Contacts button is present, click **Tools** and then **Options**. The Options dialog box appears with the Preferences tab displayed; click **Contact Options**. The Contact Options dialog box appears; click the **Show Contact Linking on All Forms** check box (☐ changes to ☑).

View a Journal Entry

You can easily view a journal entry in order to review related activities. To view a journal entry, you must first switch to Journal view in Outlook; one way to do so is to click Go and then Journal. Another is to click the Journal button at the bottom of the navigation pane.

VIEW AN ENTRY FROM WITHIN JOURNAL

1. Click the **Journal** button (🗒) at the bottom of the navigation pane to switch to Journal view.

   Outlook displays your journal entries on a timeline.

2. Right-click the entry you want to open.

3. Click **Open**.

Outlook opens the journal entry in its own window.

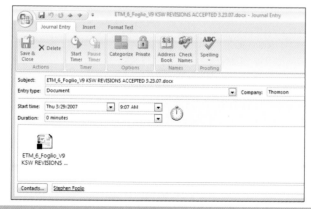

VIEW AN ENTRY FROM WITHIN CONTACTS

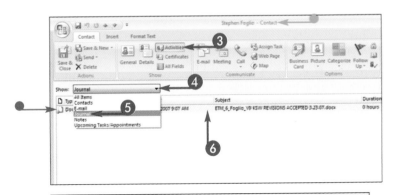

1. Click the **Contacts** button in the navigation pane to switch to Contacts view.

2. Double-click the contact whose journal entries you want to see.

● Outlook opens the contact in its own window.

3. Click **Activities**.

4. Click the **Show** [▾].

5. Click **Journal**.

● Outlook displays journal entries that are associated with the contact.

6. Double-click a journal entry.

Outlook opens the journal entry in its own window.

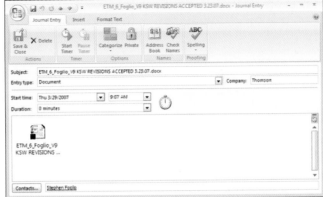

 TIPS

Where is the Journal button?

If the Journal button (🖪) does not appear at the bottom of the navigation pane, click [▾] in the bottom-right corner of the pane, choose **Add or Remove Buttons**, and select **Journal**.

Can I sort journal entries?

You can sort journal entries by clicking a different view option (◎ changes to ●) under Current View on the navigation pane. For example, you can sort entries by contact, category, and more (●).

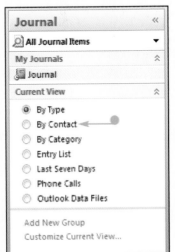

Print a Journal Entry

You can print your Outlook journal entries. In addition to printing individual entries, you can print a list of entries, provided the notes are displayed in Entry List view. You might print a journal entry to pass it on to someone else.

① If necessary, click the **Journal** button (⬜) at the bottom of the navigation pane to switch to Journal view.

② Right-click the journal entry you want to print.

③ Click **Open**.

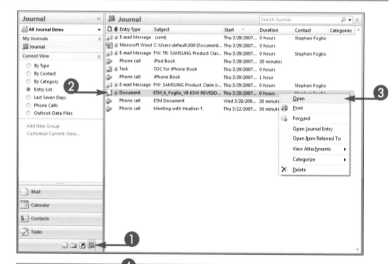

The journal entry appears.

④ Click the **Print Preview** button (⬜) in the Quick Access toolbar to preview the printout.

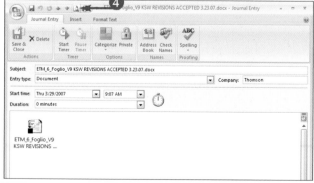

Outlook displays a preview of the printout.

⑤ Review the layout of the journal entry.

⑥ Click the **Print** button.

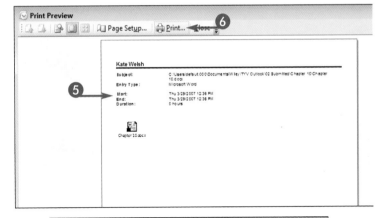

The Print dialog box appears.

⑦ Select the printer you want to use.

⑧ To print any attachments associated with the journal entry, click the **Print Attached Files** check box (☐ changes to ☑).

⑨ Type the number of copies you want to print.

⑩ If you are printing multiple copies, and you want them to be collated, click the **Collate Copies** check box (☐ changes to ☑).

⑪ Click **OK** to print the contact.

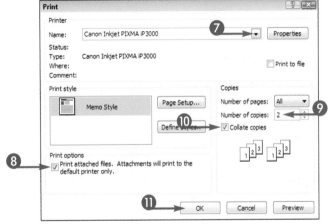

TIPS

Is there a quicker way to print a journal entry?

If you know you do not need to set printer options, and can instead use the default printer settings, you can bypass the Print dialog box, sending your journal entry straight to the printer. To do so, right-click the journal entry in Journal view and click **Print** from the menu that appears.

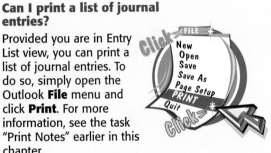

Can I print a list of journal entries?

Provided you are in Entry List view, you can print a list of journal entries. To do so, simply open the Outlook **File** menu and click **Print**. For more information, see the task "Print Notes" earlier in this chapter.

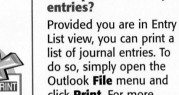

Managing Outlook

The sheer volume of information handled by Outlook — e-mail messages, calendar entries, contacts, tasks, notes, journal entries, and so on — can easily overwhelm any user. To help you deal with all this information, Outlook includes several management features, including search functionality, color categories, and more.

Create a Folder

Suppose you frequently receive e-mail messages from the same source. To keep those messages organized, you can place them in their own folder, which you create. Folders can also hold other Outlook items.

Create a Folder

1. Click **File**.
2. Click **New**.
3. Click **Folder**.

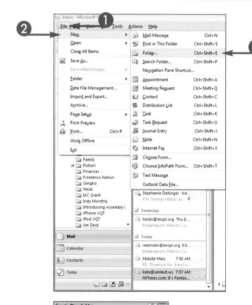

The Create New Folder dialog box appears.

4. Type a descriptive name for the new folder.
5. Click the **Folder Contains** ▾.
6. Click the type of Outlook item the folder will contain (here, **Mail and Post Items**).

7 Click the folder in which you want the new folder to reside (here, **Inbox**).

8 Click **OK**.

● Outlook adds the folder.

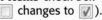

Where is the folder list?

By default, Outlook displays the folder list in the navigation pane in Mail, but not in Calendar, Contacts, Tasks, Notes, or Journal. To view the list in these other Outlook programs, click the **Folder List** button () at the bottom of the navigation pane.

How many files are in my folder?

Outlook automatically displays the number of unread items in a folder alongside that folder in the folder list. To view the total number of items in the folder, rather than just the number of unread items, right-click the folder and choose **Properties**; then, on the General tab, click the **Show Total Number of Items** check box (☐ changes to ☑).

Add a Folder to Your Favorites

At the top of the folder list in Mail's navigation pane is a set of favorite Mail folders. You can add folders you use regularly to this list to make them easier to find. Folders in the Favorite Folders group remain visible when the navigation pane is minimized and can be arranged in whatever order you like.

Add a Folder to Your Favorites

ADD A FOLDER TO THE FAVORITE FOLDERS GROUP

① Right-click the folder you want to add to the Favorite Folders group.

② Click **Add to Favorite Folders**.

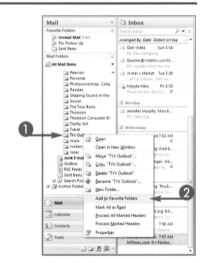

● The folder is copied to the Favorite Folders group.

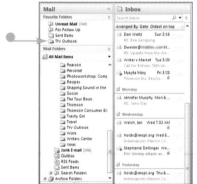

REMOVE A FOLDER FROM THE FAVORITE FOLDERS GROUP

1 Right-click the folder you want to remove from the Favorite Folders group.

2 Click **Remove from Favorite Folders**.

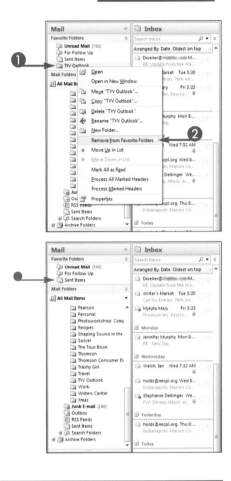

● The folder is removed from the Favorite Folders group.

How do I rearrange folders in Favorite Folders?

If you use one folder more than the others, you can bump it to the top of your Favorite Folders list. To do so, right-click the folder in Favorite Folders and click **Move Up in List**. Likewise, bump the folder down in the list by clicking **Move Down in List**.

How do I minimize the navigation pane?

As mentioned, only those folders in the Favorite Folders group (●) remain visible when the navigation pane is minimized. To minimize the navigation pane, click the « button; redisplay the pane in full by clicking the » button that replaces it.

File an E-mail Message in a Folder

After you create a folder in Outlook, you can move e-mail messages into that folder, much the way you file papers in file folders to keep them organized.

File an E-mail Message in a Folder

① Right-click the e-mail message you want to file.

② Click **Move to Folder**.

The Move Items dialog box appears.

③ Click the folder into which you want to move the selected message.

④ Click **OK**.

● The message is removed from the
message list.

⑤ To verify that the message was moved,
click the folder you chose in Step **3** in
the folder list.

● The message appears in the message list.

TIPS

**Is there a faster way
to file an e-mail
message?**

Another way to file an
e-mail message is to
simply click and
drag it from the
message list to
the folder list to
the folder to which
you want to move it.

**Can I copy, rather than
move, a message to a
folder?**

To copy, rather
than move, a
message to a
folder, hold down
the `Ctrl` key on
your keyboard as
you drag the file to
the desired folder.

Work with
Outlook Offline

If you use a dial-up connection, you might want to work in Outlook offline in order to avoid incurring charges, composing messages to be sent upon connection. You can configure Outlook to automatically connect to the Internet in order to send messages you compose offline — and retrieve incoming messages — at the interval you specify.

Work with Outlook Offline

SWITCH TO OFFLINE MODE

① Click **File**.

② Click **Work Offline**.

A check mark appears next to the File menu's Work Offline command and Outlook switches to offline mode.

SWITCH TO ONLINE MODE

① Click **File**.

② Click **Work Offline**.

The check mark next to the File menu's Work Offline command is removed, and Outlook switches to online mode.

ESTABLISH OFFLINE SEND/RECEIVE SETTINGS

1 Click **Tools**.

2 Click **Send/Receive**.

3 Click **Send/Receive Settings**.

4 Click **Define Send/Receive Groups**.

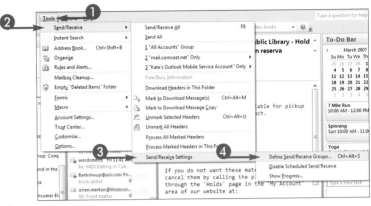

The Send/Receive Groups dialog box appears.

5 Click the Send/Receive group to which you want these settings to apply.

6 Under When Outlook Is Offline, click the **Schedule an Automatic Send/Receive Every x Minutes** check box (☐ changes to ☑).

7 Type the interval, in minutes, at which the automatic Send/Receive operation should occur.

8 Click **Close**.

Your offline Send/Receive preferences are applied.

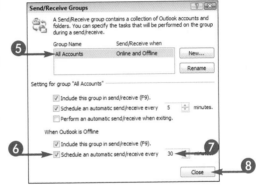

TIPS

What about my RSS subscriptions?

In addition to sending any e-mail messages you compose offline and retrieving incoming messages, the automatic Send/Receive operation also checks for updates to any RSS feeds and Internet calendars to which you have subscribed, as well as updates to any SharePoint resources you are set up to use. See Chapter 7 for more about RSS feeds.

What is a Send/Receive Group?

By default, during a Send/Receive operation, Outlook checks all accounts you have established — multiple e-mail accounts, RSS feeds, Internet calendars, and so on. If you only want Outlook to check certain accounts, you can group those accounts and apply the Send/Receive settings to the group. To create a new group, click **New** in the Send/Receive Groups dialog box, type a name for the new group, and in the dialog box that appears choose the accounts you want the group to include (●). Then, in Step **5**, choose the new group when establishing your offline Send/Receive settings.

Categorize an Outlook Item

If several Outlook items pertain to a particular project, company, and so on, you can create a category for those items. Outlook items in the same category are color-coded. The process for categorizing an Outlook item is essentially the same regardless of what type of item it is — e-mail message, calendar entry, and so on.

Categorize an Outlook Item

CREATE A NEW CATEGORY

1. Click an Outlook item you want to place in the new category.

2. Click **Actions**.

3. Click **Categorize**.

4. Click **All Categories**.

5. In the Color Categories dialog box, click **New**.

6. In the Add New Category dialog box, type a name for the new category.

7. Click the **Color** ⏷ and select the color you want to associate with the category.

8. Click the **Shortcut Key** ⏷ and choose a shortcut key to associate with the category.

Note: *If you associate a shortcut key with a category, then you can simply press that key combination to apply the category to a selected Outlook item.*

9. Click **OK**.

10. Click **OK**.

Outlook creates the new category and applies it to the selected Outlook item.

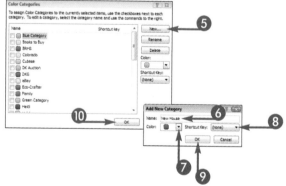

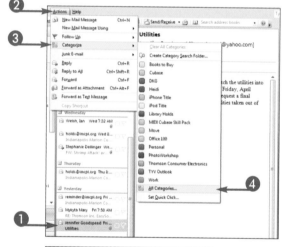

ASSIGN AN EXISTING CATEGORY TO AN OUTLOOK ITEM

1 Right-click the item you want to categorize.

2 Click **Categorize**.

3 Select the desired category from the list that appears.

● The Categorize submenu contains only the 15 categories used most recently. If the category you want to apply does not appear in the list, click **All Categories** and select the desired category in the Color Categories dialog box that appears.

● Outlook categorizes and color-codes the selected item.

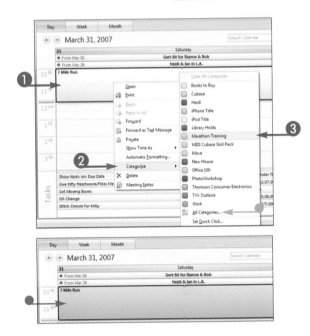

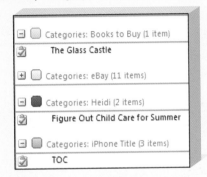

TIPS

Is there a faster way to categorize an Outlook item?

If you frequently use the same category, or need to add several items to a category in one sitting, you can use Outlook's Quick Click feature. To do so, click **Set Quick Click** in the Categorize submenu and, in the Set Quick Click dialog box that appears, click ▾ and select the category you want Quick Click to apply (●). To use Quick Click to apply the selected category, simply click an Outlook item's Categories column. (Note that Quick Click does not work with Calendar, because no Categories column is present.) To turn off Quick Click, simply choose **No Category** in the Set Quick Click dialog box.

How do I sort by category?

One of the best things about categorizing Outlook items 'is that you can then sort them by category. To sort tasks and contacts by category, click the **By Category** option (◯ changes to ◉) under Current View in the navigation pane. To sort e-mail messages, click the Arranged By heading at the top of the message list and choose **Categories**. (Note that Calendar entries cannot be sorted by category.)

Mark an Outlook Item as Private

If others are allowed access to your Outlook, you can opt to mark certain appointments or tasks as private. This prevents others from seeing details about those items. If you mark a calendar entry private, you can still convey to those who share your calendar that you are busy during the private appointment without revealing specifics about the entry.

Mark an Outlook Item as Private

MARK AN OUTLOOK ITEM AS PRIVATE

① Double-click the calendar or task entry you want to mark as private.

The Outlook item opens in its own window.

② Click the **Private** button.

③ Click **Save & Close**.

The item is marked private.

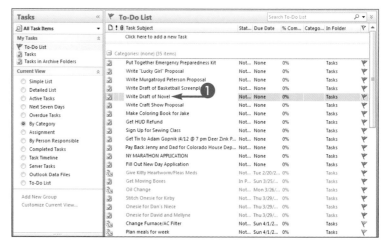

INDICATE "BUSY" STATUS

1 Double-click the private calendar entry.

● The lock icon in the bottom-right corner of the entry indicates that it is private.

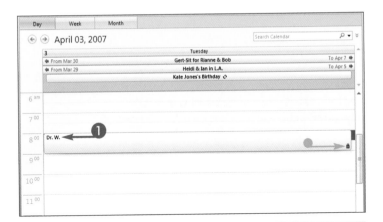

The calendar entry opens in its own window.

2 Click the **Show As** ▼.

3 Click **Busy** or **Out of Office**.

4 Click **Save & Close**.

The item is marked private.

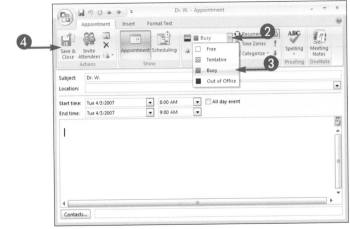

 TIPS

Are my private items really private?

Although marking an item as private prevents those with network access to your Outlook files from seeing it, it is possible for those with access to use nefarious programmatic means to view them. For this reason, you should share your Outlook files over a network only with people you really trust.

Can I keep e-mail messages private?

Although you cannot mark an e-mail message as private, you can store private e-mail messages in a folder to which others are not allowed access. To mark a folder off-limits, right-click it in the folder list and choose **Properties**; then, in the Properties dialog box's Administration tab, click the **Owners Only** button under This Folder Is Available To.

Search for Outlook Items

If you misplace an Outlook item, you can use the program's search tools to find it. One approach is to use the Instant Search box found near the top of the Mail, Calendar, Contacts, and Tasks windows to search for an e-mail message, calendar entry, contact, or task, respectively. Outlook's Query Builder function enables you to narrow your search.

Search for Outlook Items

CONDUCT AN INSTANT SEARCH

① Click the button in the navigation pane to switch to the desired Outlook program (here, **Mail**).

Note: If you are searching for an e-mail message, click the folder that contains the message you seek.

② Begin typing a keyword in the Instant Search field, located above the message list.

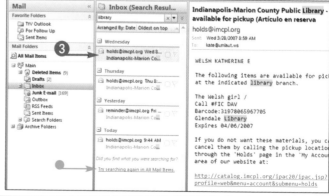

As you type, Outlook displays items that match your criterion.

③ When you see the item you want, double-click it to open it.

● If your search does not yield the desired results, try expanding it to comb through more folders. To do so, click the **Try Searching Again in All x Folders** link at the bottom of the message list that contains your search results.

USE THE QUERY BUILDER

1 Click the button in the navigation pane to switch to the desired Outlook program (here, **Tasks**).

2 Click ⊼ to the right of the Instant Search field.

● Outlook displays the Query Builder, which you can use to narrow your search.

Note: *The fields available in the Query Builder vary depending on what Outlook program you have open.*

3 Type a keyword in the Instant Search field.

4 Enter the necessary criteria in the Query Builder.

Outlook displays items that match your criterion.

5 When you see the item you want, double-click it to open it.

Can I change the fields in Query Builder?

To select different search criteria in Query Builder, click the down arrow next to the field's name and select the criterion you want. To add more criteria, click the **Add Criteria** button and select the desired criteria from the list that appears.

Can I repeat a search?

Outlook saves your ten most recent searches, enabling you to conduct them again without having to enter all the necessary information. To reuse a search, click the down arrow to the right of the Instant Search field, click **Recent Searches** (●), and select the search you want to reuse.

Create a Custom Search Folder

A search folder is a folder that contains e-mail messages that match various search criteria. By default, Outlook includes three search folders: Unread Mail, Categorized Mail, and Large Mail, placing copies of any messages that meet the established criteria in those folders. You can create your own custom search folders to store messages that meet criteria you set.

Create a Custom Search Folder

① In Mail, click **File**.

② Click **New**.

③ Click **Search Folder**.

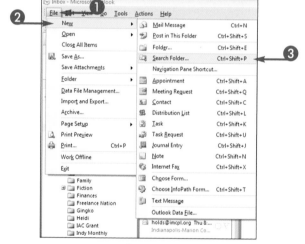

● The New Search Folder dialog box appears.

④ Under Custom, click **Create a Custom Search Folder**.

⑤ Click **Choose**.

● The Custom Search Folder dialog box appears.

⑥ Type a name for the custom search folder.

⑦ Click **Criteria** to open the Search Folder Criteria dialog box.

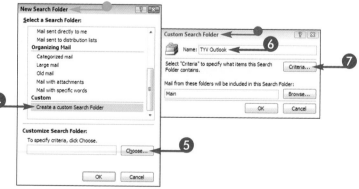

254

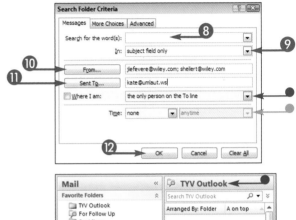

8 To search for messages that contain a certain word, type the word.

9 Choose where in the message the word you typed should appear.

10 To search for messages from a particular person, click **from** and choose the person from the dialog box that appears.

11 To search for messages addressed to a particular person, click **Sent To** and choose the person from the dialog box that appears.

● To search for messages in which your name appears in a certain line, select **Where I Am** and then choose the desired criterion.

● Use these fields to narrow the messages saved to a specific time frame.

12 Click **OK** to close the Search Folder Criteria, Custom Search Folder, and New Search Folder dialog boxes.

● Outlook creates the custom search folder and populates it with messages that match your criteria.

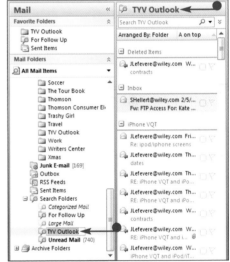

How do I search for mail in a different folder?

If you want to search for mail in a folder other than the one listed in the Custom Search Folder dialog box, click **Browse** and locate the desired folder.

Are there other types of search folders?

In addition to adding custom search folders, you can add predefined search folders, such as one for messages from specific people, or another for mail you flag for follow-up. To do so, simply click the desired predefined folder (●) in the New Search Folder dialog box and add the customization information as needed (●).

Password-Protect Outlook Information

Although Outlook does not overtly support the use of passwords per se, there are a few steps you can take to keep your Outlook information private. One is to require a password to log on to Windows; another is to password-protect your PST file — that is, the file that stores your messages and other Outlook data.

Password-Protect Outlook Information

① Click **File**.

② Click **Data File Management**.

The Account Settings dialog box appears with the Data Files tab displayed.

③ Click the PST file you want to password-protect.

④ Click **Settings** to open the Personal Folders dialog box.

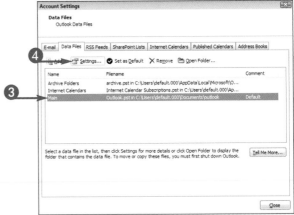

5 Click **Change Password** to open the Change Password dialog box.

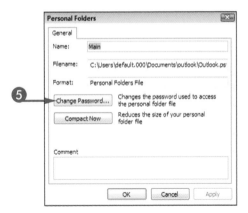

6 If you had formerly set a password, type it here; if not, skip to Step **7**.

7 Type the password you want to use here.

8 Retype the password to confirm it.

9 If you do not want to have to type your password each time you access this PST file, select **Save this Password in Your Password List**.

Note: If others have access to your computer, leave this check box unchecked; otherwise, they will be able to view the contents of your PST file.

10 Click **OK** to close the Change Password dialog box.

11 Click **OK** to close the Personal Folders dialog box.

12 Click **Close** to close the Account Settings dialog box.

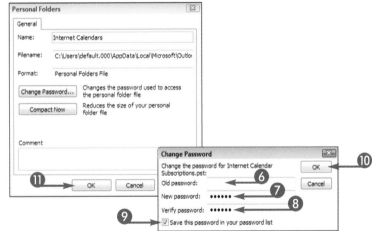

How do I set a Windows password?

To password-protect your Windows account, click **Start**, **Control Panel**, **User Accounts**, click **User Accounts** again, then **Create a Password for Your Account**, and follow the on-screen instructions. (Note that these instructions apply for Windows Vista; if you use a different version of Windows, view your version's help documentation.)

What constitutes a strong password?

To make it difficult for others to guess your password, combine uppercase and lowercase letters with numbers and symbols and use at least eight characters. Be sure to write down your password and keep it somewhere safe and private.

Use Trust Center to Keep Outlook Safe

Office includes a new feature called Trust Center that is designed to help you view and change security-related settings. These include e-mail security settings, settings for handling attachments, and settings for how downloads should be handled.

Use Trust Center to Keep Outlook Safe

① Click **Tools**.

② Click **Trust Center**.

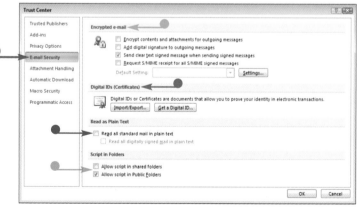

The Trust Center window opens.

③ Click **E-mail Security**.

The E-mail Security screen opens. (The default settings are shown here.)

● Change settings relating to encryption here.

● Change settings relating to digital IDs here.

● To read mail in plain text rather than HTML, click the **Read All Standard Mail in Plain Text** check box (changes to ✓).

● Use these options to specify whether scripts should be allowed to run.

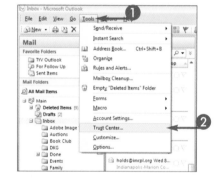

Note: A script is a type of file that can be executed without user input, making them perfect for spreading viruses.

④ Click **Attachment Handling**.

The Attachment Handling screen opens. (The default settings are shown here.)

● Click here to enable Outlook's Reply with Changes feature (☐ changes to ☑).

● Click here to disable attachment previewing (☐ changes to ☑).

⑤ Click **Automatic Download**.

The Automatic Download screen opens. (The default settings are shown here.)

● Click here if you do not want Outlook to automatically download pictures in HTML messages or RSS fields (☐ changes to ☑).

● Click these check boxes to specify any desired exceptions.

⑥ Click **OK**.

Outlook applies your Trust Center settings.

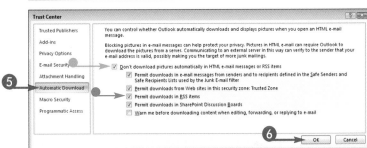

 TIPS

What is a digital ID?
Digital IDs enable more secure communication. Using a digital ID enables the sender to confirm his or her identity to the recipient via a digital certificate (similar to a computerized version of a driver's license) and to prevent others from tampering with messages.

What is Reply with Changes?
Reply with Changes is a feature that enables Outlook users collaborating on a project to keep track of changes made to a document even as it is sent back and forth among team members. For security reasons, this feature is disabled by default.

Diagnose a Problem with Office Diagnostics

On occasion, you may experience problems while running Outlook (or any other Office product). For example, your computer might crash. In the event this happens, you can run Office Diagnostics to try to diagnose and repair the problem. If you cannot get Outlook or another Office product to run, you can launch Office Diagnostics from Windows.

Diagnose a Problem with Office Diagnostics

1 Click **Help**.

2 Click **Office Diagnostics**.

Outlook launches Office Diagnostics.

3 Click **Continue**.

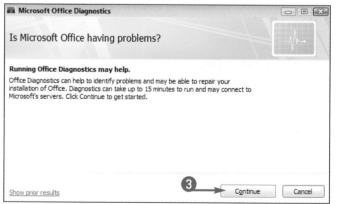

④ Click **Run Diagnostics**.

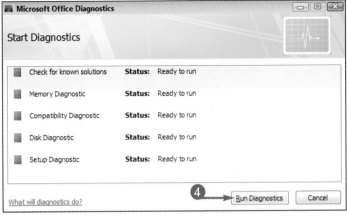

The diagnostic process begins.

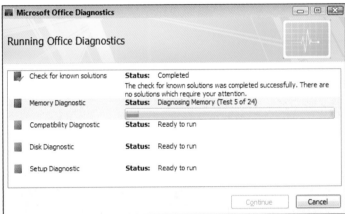

TIP

What if I cannot start an Office program to launch Office Diagnostics?

To launch Office Diagnostics from your Windows Start menu, do the following:

① Click **Start**.

② Click **All Programs**.

③ Click **Microsoft Office**.

④ Click **Microsoft Office Tools**.

⑤ Click **Microsoft Office Diagnostics**.

Office Diagnostics launches.

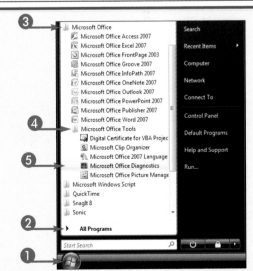

If you use Outlook with any regularity, you quickly discover that the sheer volume of e-mail messages, calendar entries, and other Outlook items can prove overwhelming. To mitigate this, Outlook automatically archives old files. If the default settings for this automatic operation do not suit you, you can change them. You can also archive items manually.

Archive Outlook Files

CHANGE AUTOARCHIVE SETTINGS

1️⃣ Click **Tools**.

2️⃣ Click **Options** to open the Options dialog box.

3️⃣ Click the **Other** tab.

4️⃣ Click **AutoArchive**.

5️⃣ In the AutoArchive dialog box, select the **Run AutoArchive Every x Days** check box and type the desired interval.

6️⃣ Select the **Archive or Delete Old Items** check box.

⦿ Click here to display the archive folder in the folder list.

7️⃣ Indicate how old an Outlook item must be to be archived.

8️⃣ Click **Move Old Items To** and choose where old items should be stored.

9️⃣ Click **Apply these Settings to All Folders Now**.

🔟 Click **OK** to close the AutoArchive dialog box.

1️⃣1️⃣ Click **OK** to close the Options dialog box.

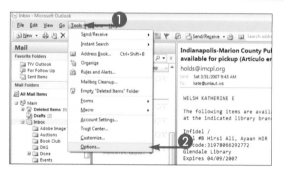

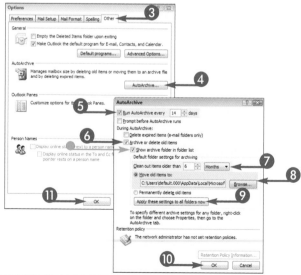

ARCHIVE ITEMS MANUALLY

1 Click **File**.

2 Click **Archive**.

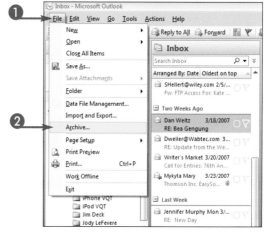

3 In the Archive dialog box, select an archive option.

● To archive all Outlook folders, click **Archive All Folders According to Their AutoArchive Settings**.

● To archive only a specific folder, click **Archive this Folder and All Subfolders**.

● If you opt to archive only a specific folder, click the folder in the list.

4 Click the **Archive Items Older Than** ☐ and choose the desired date.

● Click here to archive even those items with Do Not AutoArchive status.

● Click here to choose the folder in which the archive should be stored.

5 Click **OK**.

Outlook runs the AutoArchive operation.

Can I change archive settings for a particular folder?

When you change AutoArchive settings from the Options dialog box, the settings apply to all Outlook folders. To change the AutoArchive settings for a single folder only, do the following:

1 Click **Go**.

2 Click **Folder List**.

3 Right-click the folder whose AutoArchive settings you want to change.

4 Click **Properties**.

5 In the Properties dialog box, click the **AutoArchive** tab.

6 Change the settings as needed, and then click **OK**.

View and Restore Archived Files

You can view archived items from the Archive Folders entry in your folder list. In addition to viewing archived items, you can also restore archived items back to their original folder or to a different folder, either individually or as a group.

View and Restore Archived Files

VIEW ARCHIVED FILES

① Click **Archive Folders** in the folder list.

● If the folder list is not displayed, click **Go** and then **Folder List** to open it.

② Navigate to the folder that contains the item you want to view and click it to open it.

③ Click the item.

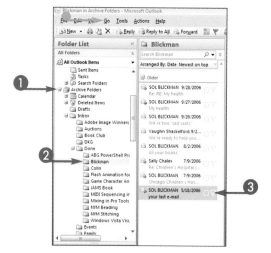

Outlook displays the message's contents in a new window.

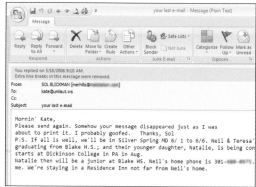

RESTORE AN ARCHIVED FILE

① Click **Archive Folders** in the folder list.

● If the folder list is not displayed, click **Go** and then **Folder List** to open it.

② Navigate to the folder that contains the message you want to restore and click it to open it.

③ Click the item you want to restore.

④ Drag the item to its original folder in the folder list.

Outlook returns the file to its original folder.

⑤ To verify that the item was moved, click the original folder.

● The item appears.

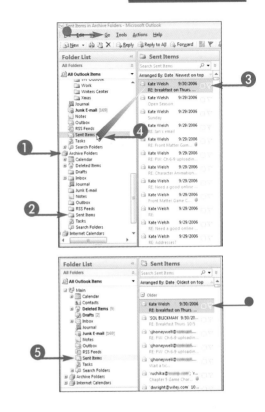

Can I restore more than one archived file at once?

To restore an entire archived folder, use the Import and Export Wizard. To launch the wizard, click **File** and then **Import and Export**; then select **Import from Another Program or File**, click **Next**, choose **Personal Folder File (.pst)** (●), click **Next**, and follow the on-screen instructions.

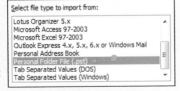

Can I disable AutoArchive?

To completely disable AutoArchive, click **Tools** and then **Options**. In the Options dialog box, click the **Other** tab, and click **AutoArchive**. Finally, in the AutoArchive dialog box, deselect the **Run AutoArchive Every *x* Days** check box. To prevent AutoArchive from running on a particular folder, right-click the folder in the folder list, click **Properties**, the **AutoArchive** tab, and select **Do Not Archive Items in This Folder**.

Delete Outlook Items

In addition to archiving e-mail messages, calendar entries, and other Outlook items, you can simply delete them. You can configure Outlook to delete outdated items automatically using AutoArchive. You can also delete Outlook items manually.

Delete Outlook Items

DELETE OUTLOOK ITEMS AUTOMATICALLY

① Click **Tools**.

② Click **Options**.

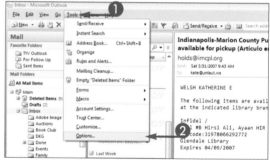

③ In the Options dialog box, click the **Other** tab.

④ Click **AutoArchive**.

⑤ In the AutoArchive dialog box, select the **Run AutoArchive Every *x* Days** check box and type the desired interval.

⑥ Select the **Delete Expired Items** check box.

⑦ Select the **Archive or Delete Old Items** check box.

⑧ Indicate how old an Outlook item must be to be deleted.

⑨ Select **Permanently Delete Old Items**.

⑩ Click **Apply these Settings to All Folders Now**.

⑪ Click **OK** to close the AutoArchive dialog box.

⑫ Click **OK** to close the Options dialog box.

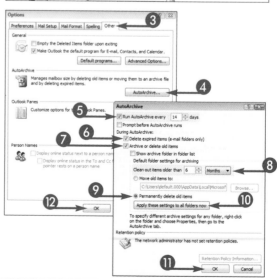

DELETE AN OUTLOOK ITEM MANUALLY

① Right-click the Outlook item you want to delete.

② Click **Delete**.

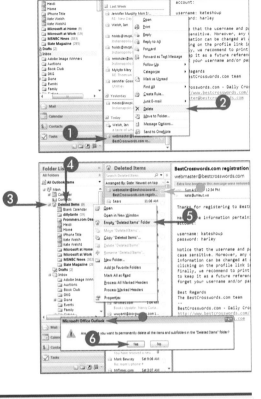

Outlook moves the item to the Deleted Items folder.

③ To verify that the file has been moved to the Deleted Items folder, click **Deleted Items** in the folder list.

● The item appears.

④ To permanently remove the item from your system, you must empty the Deleted Items folder. To begin, right-click **Deleted Items**.

⑤ Click **Empty "Deleted Items" Folder**.

● Outlook prompts you to confirm the operation.

⑥ Click **Yes**.

 TIPS

Can I change delete settings for a particular folder?

When you change AutoArchive's delete settings from the Options dialog box, the settings apply to all Outlook folders. To change the delete settings for a single folder only, right-click the folder in the folder list whose delete settings you want to change, click **Properties**, click the **AutoArchive** tab in the dialog box that appears, click the **Archive this Folder Using these Settings** option (◎ changes to ◉), and click the **Permanently Delete Old Items** option (◎ changes to ◉).

Can I manually delete multiple items at once?

To select multiple items for deletion, hold down the Ctrl key on your keyboard as you click the items you want to delete. Then right-click any of the selected items and click **Delete** (●) from the menu that appears.

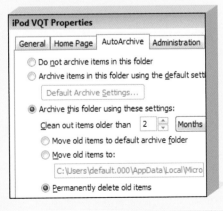

Customizing Outlook

Microsoft recognizes that everyone has a different way of working, which is why it designed Outlook to be customizable. For example, you can change options relating to each of the components in Outlook, as well as adjust Outlook's interface to better suit your needs.

Hide and Display Ribbon Commands

In lieu of using the traditional menu system and toolbars, many Outlook windows feature what Microsoft calls the *Ribbon*, which groups related commands, placing them under clickable tabs. If you feel the Ribbon consumes too much space in your Outlook windows, you can hide it, displaying it only when it is needed.

Hide and Display Ribbon Commands

HIDE THE RIBBON

1 With an Outlook window that contains a Ribbon open, such as a new message window, click ⊽ in the Quick Access toolbar.

Outlook displays the Customize Quick Access Toolbar menu.

2 Click **Minimize the Ribbon**.

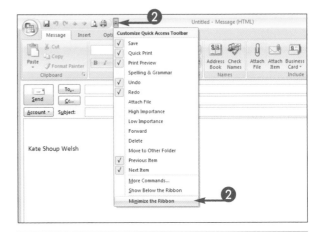

Outlook adds a check mark next to the Minimize the Quick Access toolbar's Minimize the Ribbon command and hides the Ribbon.

● Notice that the Ribbon's tabs are still present; to reveal options in a tab, click it; hide the options again by clicking the tab a second time.

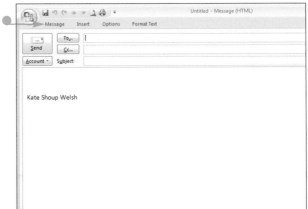

DISPLAY THE RIBBON

① Click ⊡ in the Quick Access toolbar.

Outlook displays the Customize Quick Access Toolbar menu.

② Click **Minimize the Ribbon**.

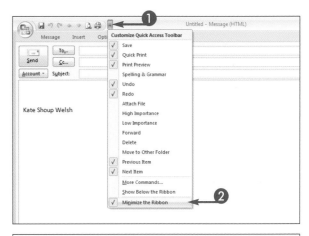

Outlook removes the check mark next to the Minimize the Quick Access toolbar's Minimize the Ribbon command and displays the Ribbon.

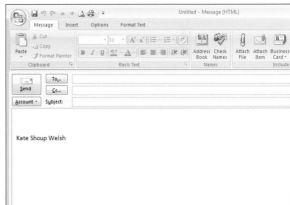

TIPS

Is there a faster way to minimize the Ribbon?

To quickly minimize the Ribbon, double-click any of its tabs. To redisplay it, double-click a tab a second time.

Can I hide the Ribbon and display the traditional menus and toolbar instead?

You cannot replace the Ribbon in Office 2007 with the menus and toolbars found in previous versions of Office.

Customize the Quick Access Toolbar

The Quick Access toolbar, found in certain Outlook windows, offers easy access to often-used commands such as Save and Quick Print. Various program-specific commands are also available; for example, in Mail windows, the Quick Access toolbar includes Mail-related commands, but includes Calendar-related options in Calendar windows. You can customize the Quick Access toolbar to change what commands are available.

Customize the Quick Access Toolbar

① With an Outlook window that contains a Ribbon open, such as a new message window, click ⬇ in the Quick Access toolbar.

Outlook displays the Customize Quick Access Toolbar menu.

② Click the command you want to add to the toolbar.

● A button for the selected command appears.

In this example, **Spelling & Grammar** is selected.

③ If you do not find the command you want to add, click ⬇ in the Quick Access toolbar.

④ Click **More Commands**.

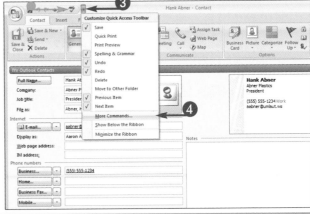

The Editor Options window opens with Quick Access toolbar options displayed.

5 Click the command you want to add.

Note: *If the command you want to add is not displayed, click the **Choose Commands From** ▾ and select **All Commands**.*

6 Click **Add**.

7 Click **OK**.

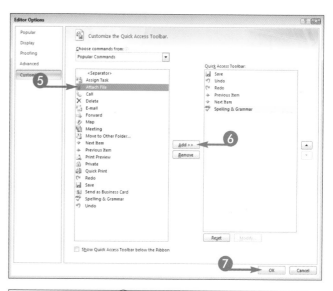

● A button for the selected command appears.

In this example, **Attach File** is selected.

Is there a quicker way to add a command to the Quick Access toolbar?

If you want to add a command that appears on the Ribbon to the Quick Access toolbar, right-click the command on the Ribbon and click **Add to Quick Access Toolbar** from the menu that appears.

Can I move the Quick Access toolbar?

You can situate the Quick Access toolbar below the Ribbon instead of at its default location above the Ribbon. To do so, click ▾ in the Quick Access toolbar and choose **Show Below the Ribbon** from the menu that appears.

Customize Outlook Today

Outlook Today displays an overview of the day's appointment and tasks, as well as how many e-mail messages you have. You can change the particulars of what is displayed in Outlook Today.

Customize Outlook Today

1 Click **Customize Outlook Today**.

The Customize Outlook Today screen opens.

2 To display Outlook Today whenever Outlook starts, click the **When Starting, Go Directly to Outlook Today** check box to select it.

3 To change the e-mail folders about which Outlook Today displays information, click **Choose Folders**.

4 In the Select Folder dialog box, select the check box next to each folder you want to include.

5 Click **OK**.

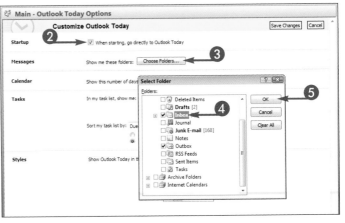

6 Click the **Show this Number of Days in My Calendar** and select the number of days you want to appear in Outlook Today.

7 Select a display option.

● If you selected Today's Tasks in Step **7** but want to view tasks for which a due date has not been set, select the **Include Tasks with No Due Date** check box.

8 Click the **Sort My Task List By** and choose the criterion by which your tasks should be sorted.

9 Select a sort order.

10 Click the **Show Outlook Today in This Style** and choose any of the pre-defined Outlook Today designs.

11 Click **Save Changes**.

Outlook applies your changes.

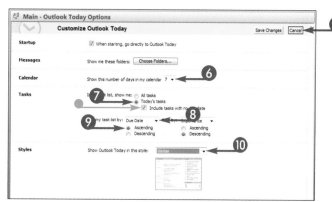

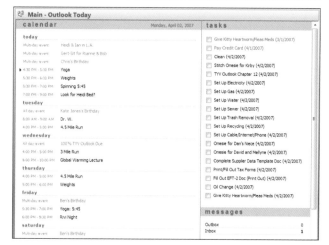

How do I open Outlook Today?

To display Outlook Today, click **Main** (●) in the folder list.

Can I access Outlook features from Outlook Today?

Conveniently, Outlook Today contains links to various Outlook features. For example, to access Tasks, click the **Tasks** link at the top of the task list in Outlook Today. Alternatively, click a task or calendar entry to open that entry.

Customize the To-Do Bar

The To-Do bar, which appears along the right side of the Outlook window by default, serves much the same purpose as Outlook Today, offering an overview of appointments, tasks, and so on. If you want, you can change the particulars of what is displayed in the To-Do bar.

Customize the To-Do Bar

① Click **View**.

② Click **To-Do Bar**.

③ Click **Options**.

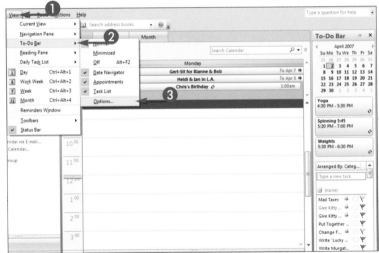

④ To display the date navigator in the To-Do bar, ensure that the **Show Date Navigator** check box is selected (changes to).

⑤ Type the number of months you want to be able to see in the To-Do bar.

⑥ To display upcoming appointments in the To-Do bar, ensure that the **Show Appointments** check box is selected (changes to).

⑦ Type the number of appointments you want to be able to see in the To-Do bar.

⑧ To display tasks in the To-Do bar, ensure that the **Show Task List** check box is selected (changes to).

⑨ Click **OK**.

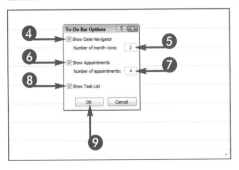

● Outlook adjusts the appearance of the To-Do bar to reflect your selections.

⑩ To minimize the To-Do bar, freeing up room for other Outlook components, click **View**.

⑪ Click **To-Do Bar**.

⑫ Click **Minimized**.

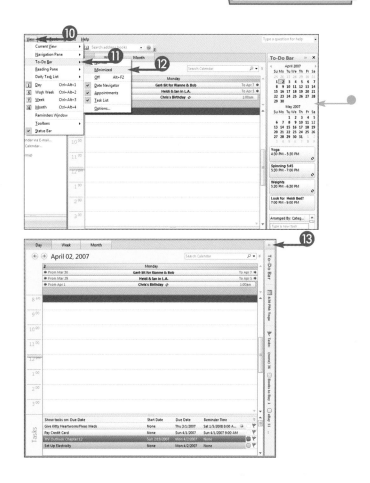

Outlook minimizes the To-Do bar.

⑬ To again reveal the To-Do bar, click ⫷.

 TIPS

Can I resize the To-Do bar?

In addition to minimizing the To-Do bar, you can also resize it to make it wider or narrower. To do so, place your mouse pointer over the left edge of the bar; when it changes to a double-sided arrow (↔), click and drag left or right to widen or narrow the To-Do bar, respectively.

Can I turn the To-Do bar off?

To turn the To-Do bar off, click **View**, **To-Do Bar**, and then **Off**. Turn it back on by clicking **View**, **To-Do Bar**, and then **Normal**.

Customize the Navigation Pane

The navigation pane appears along the left side of the Outlook screen, and contains program-specific options. For example, the options displayed when Calendar is open are different from the options that appear when Mail is active. You can customize certain aspects of the navigation pane — for example, adding, removing, or rearranging buttons or reducing its size.

1 To add, remove, or rearrange buttons, click ▼ at the bottom of the navigation pane.

2 Click **Navigation Pane Options**.

The Navigation Pane Options dialog box appears.

3 Ensure that a check box appears next to each button you want displayed in the navigation pane, and that any buttons you want to omit are unchecked.

4 To change the order in which buttons appear, click an entry in the list.

5 Click **Move Up** or **Move Down** to change the placement of the button.

6 Click **OK**.

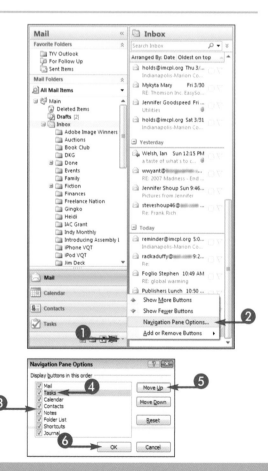

● Outlook adds, moves, and rearranges the buttons accordingly.

7 To minimize the navigation pane, freeing up room for other Outlook components, click **View**.

8 Click **Navigation Pane**.

9 Click **Minimized**.

Outlook minimizes the navigation pane.

10 To again reveal the navigation pane, click ⟪.

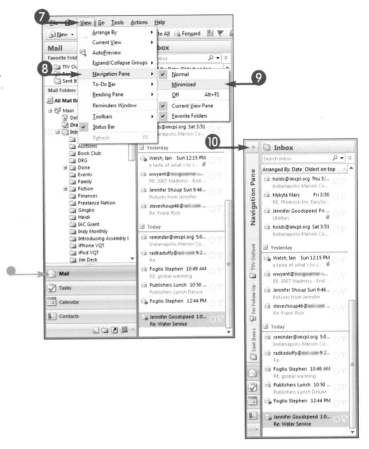

TIPS

Can I resize the navigation pane?

In addition to minimizing the navigation pane, you can also resize it to make it wider or narrower. To do so, place your mouse pointer over the left edge of the bar; when it changes to a double-sided arrow (↔), click and drag left or right to widen or narrow the navigation pane bar.

Can I turn the navigation pane off?

To turn the navigation pane off, click **View**, **Navigation Pane**, and then **Off**. Turn it back on by clicking **View**, **Navigation Pane**, and then **Normal**.

Customize the Reading Pane

The reading pane, displayed by default in Mail but not in other Outlook programs, enables you to view the contents of a message, calendar entry, contact, or task without opening it. You can display or hide the reading pane as needed, as well as specify whether it appears in the right side or bottom half of the Outlook screen.

Customize the Reading Pane

1 To display the reading pane, click **View**.

2 Click **Reading Pane**.

3 Click an orientation for the reading pane (here, **Right**).

● Outlook displays the reading pane.

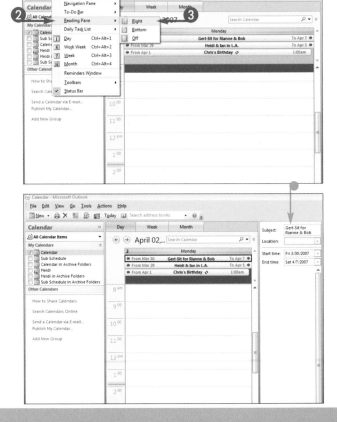

4 To change the location of the reading pane, click **View**.

5 Click **Reading Pane**.

6 Click an orientation for the reading pane (here, **Bottom**).

● Outlook moves the pane.

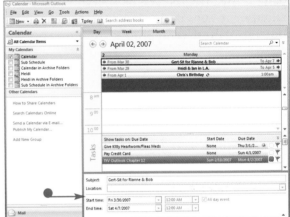

Can I resize the reading pane?

In addition to minimizing the Navigation pane, you can also resize it to make it wider or narrower. To do so, place your mouse pointer over the left edge of the bar; when it changes to a double-sided arrow (↔), click and drag left or right to widen or narrow the reading pane bar. To turn the reading pane off, click **View**, **Reading Pane**, and then **Off**. Turn it back on by clicking **View**, **Reading Pane**, and then **Normal**.

Are there more reading pane options?

In addition to establishing how the reading pane looks and where it is situated in the window, you can also configure how e-mail messages viewed in the reading pane are processed by Outlook. For example, you can configure Outlook to mark a message as Read after it has been displayed in the reading pane. To access these options, click **Tools**, **Options**, and, in the **Other** tab, click **Reading Pane**; the Reading Pane dialog box opens.

Change Which Outlook Component Launches by Default

If you consistently use a particular Outlook program right after launching Outlook — for example, Calendar — you can configure Outlook to open that program by default at start-up. This saves you the step of clicking the Calendar button in the navigation pane to switch to that program each time Outlook launches.

① Click **Tools**.

② Click **Options**.

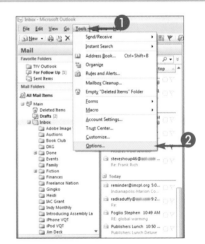

The Options dialog box appears.

③ Click the **Other** tab.

④ Click **Advanced Options**.

The Advanced Options dialog box appears.

5 Click **Browse**.

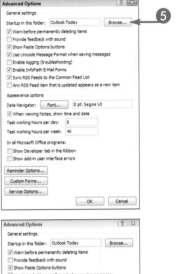

The Select Folder dialog box appears.

6 Click the folder for the Outlook component you want to launch at start-up.

7 Click **OK** to close the Select Folder dialog box.

8 Click **OK** to close the Advanced Options dialog box.

9 Click **OK** to close the Options dialog box.

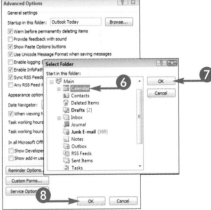

 TIPS

Can I launch a specific folder at start-up?

You are not limited to running a particular Outlook component at start-up. Indeed, you can configure Outlook to launch a certain folder. For example, you might configure the program to start Mail with the Drafts folder displayed at start-up. To do so, simply click the folder you want to launch in Step **6**.

How do I launch Outlook Today at start-up?

To launch Outlook Today at start-up, click **Main** in the Select Folder dialog box.

Set E-mail Options

You can change many aspects of how e-mail works in Outlook. For example, you can choose how Outlook handles messages you receive, how replies and forwards are handled, how frequently messages in progress are saved, what happens when new messages arrive, default settings for outgoing messages, and more.

Set E-mail Options

① Click **Tools**.

② Click **Options**.

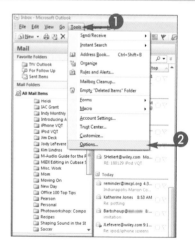

The Options dialog box appears.

③ Click **E-mail Options**.

The E-mail Options dialog box appears.

● Select how Outlook handles messages.

● Select how Outlook handles replies and forwards.

④ Click **Advanced E-mail Options**.

The Advanced E-mail Options dialog box appears.

● Select AutoSave options here.

● Specify how Outlook should behave when a new message is received.

● Indicate how Outlook should behave when sending messages.

⑤ Click **OK** to close the Advanced E-mail Options dialog box.

⑥ Click **OK** to close the E-mail Options dialog box.

⑦ Click **OK** to close the Options dialog box.

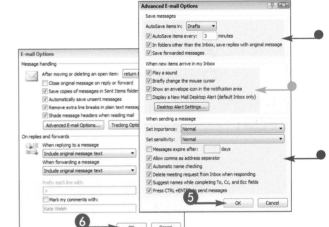

TIPS

What happens if I click Tracking Options?

Clicking **Tracking Options** in the E-mail Options dialog box opens the Tracking Options dialog box. Here, you can specify how Outlook verifies the date and time at which messages you send to others are received, as well as whether read receipts or delivery receipts should be sent. You also specify how Outlook handles requests from others for read receipts.

What e-mail options are found in the Mail Setup tab?

Click the Options dialog box's **Mail Setup** tab to set up e-mail accounts, change send and receive settings (for example, whether Outlook should perform a Send/Receive operation as soon as it is connected to the Internet), change data-file settings (*data files* are the files used to store e-mail messages), and to establish dial-up settings.

Change Spelling and AutoCorrect Options

Nothing is more embarrassing than sending a message to your boss that includes a spelling or other error. To help prevent this, Outlook includes tools for detecting and correcting errors. One is spell-check, which you can run automatically; another is AutoCorrect, which automatically corrects mistakes. To ensure best results, you can change various options for these tools.

Change Spelling and AutoCorrect Options

① Click **Tools**.

② Click **Options**.

The Options dialog box appears.

③ Click the **Spelling** tab.

④ If you want Outlook to always run a spell-check on outgoing messages, select the **Always Check Spelling Before Sending** check box.

⑤ To speed up the spell-check, select the **Ignore Original Message Text in Reply or Forward** check box. That way, only the text you add is checked.

⑥ Click **Spelling and AutoCorrection** to open the Editor Options window to the Proofing settings.

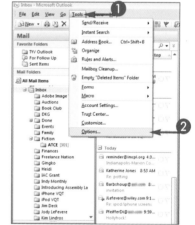

⑦ Click **AutoCorrect Options**.

⑧ In the AutoCorrect dialog box, ensure the **Replace Text as You Type** check box is selected.

⑨ Type a mistake you commonly make — for example, if you frequently type aand instead of and, type **aand** here.

⑩ Type the text that should replace the incorrect text — here, **and**.

⑪ Click **Add**.

⑫ Click **OK**.

Note: *AutoCorrect automatically corrects misspellings and other errors. If AutoCorrect erroneously corrects a word you typed, you can dismiss the change by clicking* ⬛▾ *and choosing* **Change Back To**.

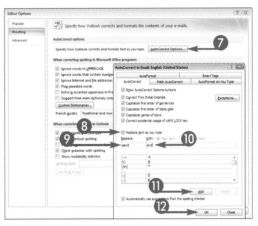

● Set additional spelling options here, such as whether repeated words should be flagged.

● Select how the spell-check operation should behave when performed in Outlook.

⑬ Click **OK**.

⑭ Click **OK** to close the Options dialog box.

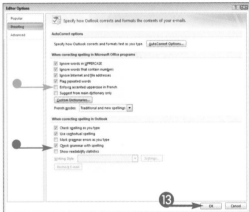

 TIPS

Can I change how Outlook formats my messages?

In addition to setting spelling and AutoCorrect options, you can also choose how text in your messages is formatted — for example, whether bulleted lists are applied automatically as you type, whether straight quotes are replaced with smart quotes, and so on. These settings are accessible from the AutoFormat As You Type and AutoFormat tabs found in the AutoCorrect dialog box.

Are there more Outlook message options?

For more options that relate to how Outlook handles text, click **Advanced** in the Editor Options window. You find settings such as whether text can be dragged and dropped, whether you can Ctrl -click to follow a hyperlink, and so on.

Set Calendar Options

You can change many Outlook Calendar settings. For example, you can choose which days constitute your workweek, what day should be listed as the first day of the week, whether week numbers should appear in Month view, and so on.

① Click **Tools**.

② Click **Options**.

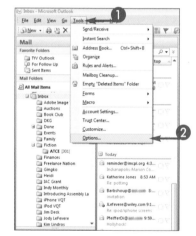

The Options dialog box appears.

③ If you want Calendar to set reminders by default, select the **Default Reminder** check box.

④ Click the **Default Reminder** ▾ and establish the default reminder interval.

⑤ Click **Calendar Options** to open the Calendar Options dialog box.

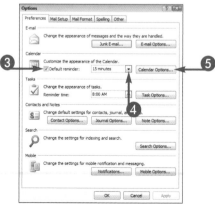

⑥ Select these check boxes to specify the workweek in Calendar.

⑦ Click the **First Day of Week** ⏷ and select the day you want to appear first when you display Calendar in Week or Month view.

⑧ Click the **First Week of Year** ⏷ and specify how Outlook should determine the first week of the year.

⑨ Click the **Start Time** ⏷ and **End Time** ⏷ to set the hours of your day.

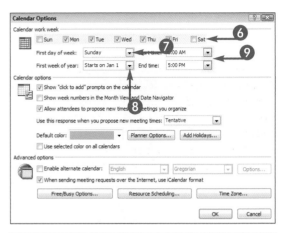

● Select the **Show "Click to Add" Prompts" on the Calendar** check box if you want Calendar to prompt you to add an appointment when you place your cursor over it.

● Use these settings to establish how Calendar handles meeting requests.

● Click the **Default Color** ⏷ to change the color of the calendar in Outlook.

⑩ Click **OK**.

⑪ Click **OK** to close the Options dialog box.

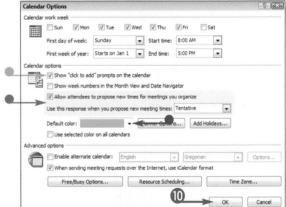

 TIP

What happens if I change my time zone?
If you change time zones in Outlook, Calendar items are updated accordingly. To change time zones, do the following:

① Repeat Steps **1** to **5** to open the Calendar Options dialog box.

② Click **Time Zone**.

③ In the Time Zone dialog box, type a name for the new time.

④ Click the **Time Zone** ⏷ and choose the desired time zone.

⑤ To instruct Outlook to automatically adjust for daylight saving time, click **Adjust for Daylight Saving Time** (☐ changes to ☑).

⑥ Click **OK** to close the dialog boxes.

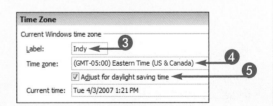

Set Tasks Options

You can change a few settings that relate to Outlook Tasks, such as the time at which Outlook reminds you of impending tasks, as well as appearance-related options such as the color of completed tasks.

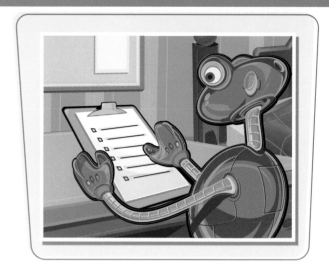

① Click **Tools**.

② Click **Options**.

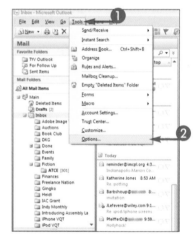

The Options dialog box appears.

③ To change the time at which Outlook sends reminders for tasks, click the **Reminder Time** ▾ and select the desired time.

④ Click **Task Options**.

The Task Options dialog box appears.

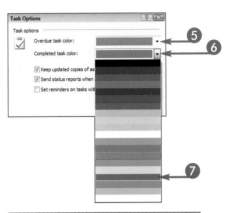

⑤ Click the **Overdue Task Color** ▾ and select the color you want applied to overdue tasks.

⑥ Click the **Completed Task Color** ▾.

⑦ Select the color you want applied to completed tasks.

● To retain copies of assigned tasks, select the **Keep Updated Copies of Assigned Tasks on My Task List** check box.

● To automatically send a status report upon completion of an assigned task, select the **Send Status Reports When Assigned Tasks are Completed** check box.

● To receive reminders for tasks with due dates, select the **Set Reminders on Tasks with Due Dates** check box.

⑧ Click **OK**.

⑨ Click **OK**.

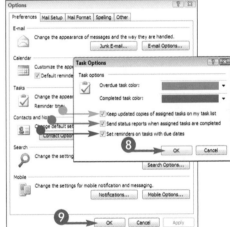

Can I view tasks in Calendar?

Calendar can display a list of tasks due on the selected day. To display the list, switch to Calendar, click **View**, **Daily Task List**, and then **Normal**. To see options relating to the task list in Calendar, click **Arrange By** in the Daily Task List submenu. (Note that tasks are visible in Calendar only in Day and Week views.)

Can I resize the columns in Tasks?

To change the size — and other characteristics — of the columns in Tasks, click **View**, **Current View**, and then **Format Columns**. In the dialog box that appears, click the name of the column you want to change (●) and make the necessary adjustments.

Set Contact Options

You can quickly and easily change how Outlook handles contacts — for example, selecting naming and filing preferences for new contacts, whether Outlook should check for duplicate contacts, and so on.

① Click **Tools**.

② Click **Options**.

● The Options dialog box appears.

③ Click **Contact Options**.

● The Contact Options dialog box appears.

④ Click the **Default "Full Name" Order** ▼ and choose how you want your contacts' full names to appear.

⑤ Click the **Default "File As" Order** ▼ and choose how contacts should be filed.

⑥ Click the **Check for Duplicate Contacts** check box (changes to ☑).

⑦ Click **OK** to close the Contact Options dialog box.

⑧ Click **OK** to close the Options dialog box.

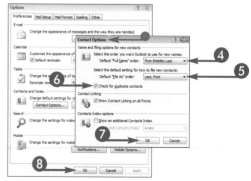

Set Note Options

Outlook includes a Note feature that it acts much like the omnipresent sticky note. You can quickly and easily change options relating to notes created with this feature, such as their color, their size, and the font used.

Set Note Options

① Click **Tools**.

② Click **Options**.

● The Options dialog box appears.

③ Click **Note Options**.

● The Notes Options dialog box appears.

④ Click the **Color** ▾ and select the default color for new notes.

⑤ Click the **Size** ▾ and select the default size for new notes.

⑥ Click **Font**.

● The Font dialog box appears.

⑦ Select a font, font style, and font size.

⑧ Click the **Color** ▾ and select a default font color.

● Review your font selections here.

⑨ Click **OK** to close the Font dialog box.

⑩ Click **OK** to close the Notes Options dialog box.

⑪ Click **OK** to close the Options dialog box.

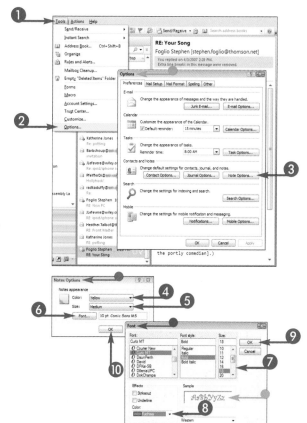

Set Search Options

Outlook's Instant Search capabilities enable you to find the Outlook items you need in a flash, be they e-mail messages, calendar entries, contacts, and so on. If you want, you can modify certain aspects of Outlook's Instant Search function, such as which folders are indexed for searching.

Set Search Options

① Click **Tools**.

② Click **Options**.

The Options dialog box appears.

③ Click **Search Options** to open the Search Options dialog box.

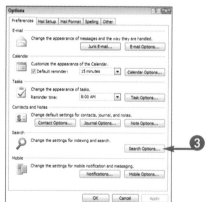

● Choose indexing settings, such as which folders you want Outlook to index and whether Outlook should notify you when searches may be incomplete.

● Choose search settings here, such as whether Outlook should display search results as you type, speed up searches by limiting the number of results shown, and or highlight words in the search criteria.

● To include items in the Deleted Items folder in search results, click here.

● Specify whether Outlook should search all folders or only the currently selected folder.

④ Click **Change**.

The Color dialog box appears.

⑤ Click the color you want to use to highlight search words.

⑥ Click **OK**.

⑦ Click **OK** to close the Search Options and Options dialog boxes.

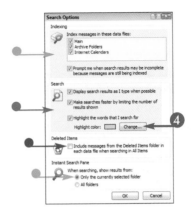

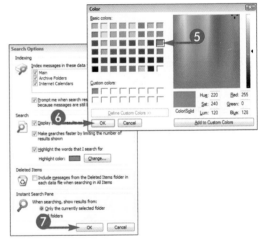

What is indexing?

As you work with Outlook, sending and receiving messages, entering contacts and calendar information, and so on, Outlook automatically indexes these entries — that is, sorts and organizes them such that if you need to search for them later, they are easier to find.

Is Instant Search enabled by default?

If you use Windows Vista, then Instant Search is enabled by default. If you use other versions of Windows, however, such as Windows XP, you may need to download the Windows Desktop Search component in order to activate Instant Search. (Outlook prompts you to download the software; alternatively, click the **Click Here to Enable Instant Search** link in the Instant Search box to start the download.)

Index

Index

Index

Index

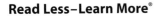

Read Less–Learn More®

There's a Visual book for every learning level...

Simplified®

The place to start if you're new to computers. Full color.

- Computers
- Mac OS
- Office
- Windows

Teach Yourself VISUALLY™

Get beginning to intermediate-level training in a variety of topics. Full color.

- Computers
- Crocheting
- Digital Photography
- Dog training
- Dreamweaver
- Excel
- Guitar
- HTML
- Knitting
- Mac OS
- Office
- Photoshop
- Photoshop Elements
- Piano
- Poker
- PowerPoint
- Scrapbooking
- Sewing
- Windows
- Wireless Networking
- Word

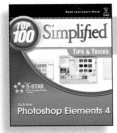

Top 100 Simplified® Tips & Tricks

Tips and techniques to take your skills beyond the basics. Full color.

- Digital Photography
- eBay
- Excel
- Google Internet
- Mac OS
- Photoshop
- Photoshop Elements
- PowerPoint
- Windows

Build It Yourself VISUALLY™

Do it yourself the visual way and without breaking the bank. Full color.

- Game PC
- Media Center PC

...all designed for visual learners—just like you!

Master VISUALLY®

Step up to intermediate-to-advanced technical knowledge. Two-color interior.

- 3ds Max
- Creating Web Pages
- Dreamweaver and Flash
- Excel VBA Programming
- iPod and iTunes
- Mac OS
- Optimizing PC Performance
- Photoshop Elements
- QuickBooks
- Quicken
- Windows
- Windows Mobile
- Windows Server

Visual Blueprint™

Where to go for professional-level programming instruction. Two-color interior.

- Ajax
- Excel Data Analysis
- Excel Pivot Tables
- Excel Programming
- HTML
- JavaScript
- Mambo
- PHP & MySQL
- Visual Basic

Visual Encyclopedia™

Your A-to-Z reference of tools and techniques. Full color.

- Dreamweaver
- Excel
- Photoshop
- Windows

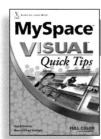

Visual Quick Tips™

Shortcuts, tricks, and techniques for getting more done in less time. Full color.

- Digital Photography
- Excel
- MySpace
- Office
- PowerPoint
- Windows
- Wireless Networking

For a complete listing of Visual books, go to wiley.com/go/visual

Visual®
An Imprint of WILEY
Now you know.